YOU
ARE THE
SENATOR

GREAT DECISIONS

YOU
ARE THE
SENATOR

Nathan Aaseng

The Oliver Press, Inc.
Minneapolis

The Oliver Press, Inc.
Charlotte Square
5707 West 36th Street
Minneapolis, MN 55416-2510

Library of Congress Cataloging-in-Publication Data

Aaseng, Nathan.
You are the senator / Nathan Aaseng.
p.   cm.—(Great decisions)
Includes bibliographical references and index.
    Summary: Examines eight historic decisions of the United
States Senate: Prohibition, the Social Security Act, the Taft-
Hartley Act, the Civil Rights Act of 1964, direct election of the
president, the War Powers Act, the Gramm-Rudman bill, and the
Brady bill.
ISBN 1-881508-36-6 (lib. bdg.)
1. United States. Congress. Senate—Decision making—Juvenile
literature.   2. United States—Politics and government—Decision
making—Juvenile literature.   3. Legislators—United States—
Juvenile literature.   [1. United States. Congress. Senate. 2.
United States—Politics and government. 3. Decision making.]   I.
Title. II. Series.
JK1276.A27 1996
328.73'077—dc20   96-4569
                                                                         CIP
                                                                          AC

ISBN: 1-881508-36-6
Great Decisions VI
Printed in the United States of America

03 02 01 00 99 98 97   8 7 6 5 4 3 2 1

CONTENTS

The Capitol Building in Washington, D.C., is home to both the Senate and the House of Representatives. Its cornerstone was laid by George Washington in 1793, but the dome and the House and Senate wings were not added until the mid-1800s.

INTRODUCTION

Welcome to the United States Senate. Your task is to join your fellow senators in passing laws that will help American society to function smoothly and fairly.

You will not have the luxury of complaining about the terrible laws and the Washington politicians who pass them. You cannot merely sit on the sidelines and criticize the senators. You are a senator. You must make a decision on each of the major issues that comes before you. You must add your vote to those cast to decide which laws will pass and which will not.

The U.S. Congress, which is made up of the Senate and the House of Representatives, is the legislative branch of the U.S. government. This means the U.S. Senate is one of only two bodies that create the federal laws that govern the entire United States of America. The other group, the House of Representatives, will vote on most of the same issues that come before you.

To make a new law, a senator or representative proposes a *bill* to the Senate or the House of Representatives.

Then the bill is debated on the floor of the Senate or the House. Before it can become a law, a bill must pass both bodies of Congress and then be signed by the president. If the president *vetoes*, or opposes, a bill, it can become a law only if two-thirds of the members of both the Senate and the House of Representatives vote to override the president's veto.

A key difference exists between the Senate and the House. The House is made up of 435 lawmakers who each represent a specific district in their home states. Each district has about the same number of *constituents*, or people who live within the district's boundaries. These

The United States Senate meets in this chamber in the north wing of the Capitol. A new session begins on January 3 of each year, and senators serve six-year terms that are staggered so only one-third of the senators are up for reelection every two years.

districts are small enough for members of Congress to represent citizens who live in one particular area. For example, a representative may serve voters primarily from an inner city, a wealthy suburb, or a rural area. The concerns of constituents from these different areas may vary greatly.

In the House, states with large populations, such as California and New York, have many representatives. States with small populations, such as Delaware and Wyoming, have as few as one. As a result, in the House, high-population states have a much greater say than low-population states in which bills become laws.

The Senate, however, consists of two senators from every state, who represent their state as a whole. This means that each state has an equal voice in deciding which laws will be made in the Senate. Also, each senator has to represent voters from every area of the state: urban, suburban, and rural. Since 1959, when Alaska and Hawaii became states, the Senate has had 100 seats.

Because the vast majority of all U.S. senators in this century have belonged to one of the two major parties, you should decide in advance whether you will be a Democrat or a Republican. As a senator, you will be representing your state and your party as the Senate tackles some of the most difficult problems that our society has faced in the twentieth century: What will you do about the tragic toll that alcoholism has taken on society? What will you do to help the huge number of elderly people who have used up their savings? How will you guarantee equal rights to all citizens? How do you prevent the president of the United States from sending American soldiers

Because the United States traditionally has had a two-party system, virtually all senators during the twentieth century have been either Democrats (whose symbol is the donkey) or Republicans (whose symbol is the elephant).

to fight wars without first seeking the approval of the American people? How do you keep the national debt from ballooning out of control?

The solutions to these problems will not be easy. You must study the background of each issue. Then you must consider a solution that lawmakers have proposed and sift through the arguments for and against the legislation. You may be asked to consider a compromise or an alternative bill.

Although a senator should be primarily concerned with what is best for the country, you will also have to consider the political cost of your various options. What kinds of pressure are activists and special-interest groups putting on you? What do your constituents think of the proposed laws? What does the political party to which you belong think of these proposals?

You may feel so strongly about some issues that you will choose a course of action without taking into account the views of the voters or of your party. You may feel less strongly about other issues. In those cases, you may want to go along with whatever solution will please the majority of the voters in your state or will best satisfy your party.

Bills brought before the Senate are easy to shoot down and difficult to pass. Fewer than 10 percent of the bills introduced in Congress ever become laws. Many senators agree with most parts of a bill but end up voting against it because they disagree with a small portion of it. You may choose to follow the same course of action. But in holding out for a more perfect law, you run the risk that no bill will pass and that the problem will not be solved.

You will learn that in a complex society, few pieces of proposed legislation will please everyone.

Your votes as a U.S. senator will become a matter of public record. Whatever your decision, the American people will hold you accountable—both for your actions and for your inaction. And Americans have traditionally not shown a great deal of patience or sympathy with their lawmakers. Now the pressure is on as you try to find solutions to some of the most difficult problems of the United States.

1

PROHIBITION
August 1917

Senator Morris Sheppard, a Democrat from Texas, has introduced into the United States Senate an amendment to the U.S. Constitution that would prohibit "the manufacture, sale, transportation, and exportation of alcoholic beverages in the United States." The amendment would also make it a federal crime to *import*, or bring in, alcohol from foreign countries.

Many states and counties have already made it illegal to distribute and sell alcoholic beverages. Numerous church leaders and women's groups as well as the Anti-Saloon League and the Prohibition Party have long sought federal legislation that would outlaw the sale and distribution of alcohol. A prohibition amendment failed to pass in 1914, but now these groups are ready to try to get it passed again.

BACKGROUND

During the first 200 years of European settlement in North America, alcoholic beverages were consumed at a far greater rate than they are now in the United States. Colonists distilled liquor from the fruits they grew and from wild berries; they also imported wines and made beers and ales from locally grown grains.

The *temperance* movement to end drinking began in the United States in the late 1700s after the popular and influential Dr. Benjamin Rush, a signer of the Declaration of Independence, started to campaign against alcohol. Rush and other early temperance activists argued that alcohol led to disease, poverty, family strife, gambling, crime, and, ultimately, to early death.

Throughout the nineteenth century, temperance groups organized locally and nationally. By 1833, in addition to the American Temperance Union, a large national temperance organization, there were 5,000 local temperance societies with more than 1 million members. Activists wrote novels and pamphlets detailing the dangers of drink. Crowds gathered to hear traveling speakers retell stories about how they descended into alcoholism and poverty and then changed their lives by not drinking alcohol any longer. Beginning in Massachusetts and Maine in the 1830s, activists called for laws that would restrict alcohol instead of simply encouraging people not to drink. Many of the greatest reformers of the nineteenth century, from black abolitionist Sojourner Truth to educator Horace Mann, were involved in the temperance movement.

In 1869, antidrinking activists, or *prohibitionists*, organized the Prohibition Party, a national political party whose goal was to ban the sale of alcohol. Beginning in the 1870s, women's groups led marches, blockaded saloons, and demonstrated at breweries to put pressure on drinkers and alcohol producers. In 1875, the Women's Christian Temperance Union began to seek a constitutional amendment for prohibition. Twenty years later, in 1895, the Anti-Saloon League, the most powerful promoter of prohibition, was organized. Wayne Wheeler, the league's leader, had a great deal of influence in political circles. He dictated legislation and told members of Congress—and even presidents—which laws to support. Although some state legislatures have been persuaded to pass laws banning the manufacture and sale of alcoholic beverages, people living in "dry" states, where the sale of alcohol is banned, can easily obtain alcohol from "wet" states that allow the sale of alcohol.

Because of the varying state laws, prohibitionists now want the U.S. Congress to pass a law that bans the manufacture and sale of alcoholic beverages in every state. But according to the United States Constitution, which spells out the powers and responsibilities of the federal government, members of Congress cannot enact such a law because doing so would interfere with the right of the states to determine their own laws. In order to pass a federal prohibition law, Congress must make the law an amendment to the Constitution.

In 1914, the Hobson-Sheppard resolution to adopt such an amendment was introduced in the House of Representatives. But unlike most bills, which require

The Prohibition Party reached its greatest popular support in 1892, when its presidential candidate, John Bidwell, won 265,000 votes.

only a simple majority vote of those present to pass in each legislative body, a constitutional amendment requires a two-thirds majority. So although a majority of law-makers actually voted for the bill, the measure did not win the necessary number of votes.

Now Senator Morris Sheppard and his allies are trying again. They have introduced the amendment and are asking for your vote.

THE DECISION IS YOURS.

How will you vote on the proposed amendment to outlaw the manufacture, sale, transportation, and exportation of alcoholic beverages in the United States?

Option 1 **Oppose the prohibition amendment.**

Although the abuse of alcoholic beverages takes a heavy toll on society, a prohibition amendment is no solution to this problem. The United States is proud of being the land of liberty, where people can pursue happiness free from excessive governmental interference. The prohibition amendment contradicts this tradition of liberty.

The enjoyment of alcohol is an individual choice. The majority of those who drink do so responsibly and cause no harm to society. In addition, this law feeds on prejudice against German Americans, who own many of the breweries, and other immigrant groups from cultures in which social drinking is important. Even though the law does not forbid people from drinking in their own homes, their right to drink responsibly will still be curtailed because it will not be legal to buy or sell alcoholic beverages. Government has no business regulating people's private choices in this way.

A second problem with the amendment is that it interferes with the rights of the states. The founders of the United States warned against concentrating too much power in the hands of a national government. They gave each state the right to make its own laws according to the will of the majority of its citizens. This includes the right to determine state laws concerning alcohol.

The network of individual state governments is working well. Those states in which a strong majority favors prohibition have already passed such laws or will pass them in response to the people's demands. Those states in which the people do not favor prohibition do not have such laws. Thus, each state is regulating its affairs by responding to the views of its citizens. Why should the people of some states live under a ban that most of them do not want?

The proposed amendment would set a dangerous example by stripping the states of their authority to make their own laws. If you allow this to happen, what other controls might the federal government want to impose on the states? What would prevent officials in the federal government from taking over even more of the states' powers?

A third argument against the amendment is that you should be cautious about amending the Constitution. The Constitution sets the framework for all government functions in the United States. It is the one and only document that protects the rights of American citizens against any government officials who might want to take away those rights. The Constitution provides stability for the entire nation. Any time you tamper with this document, you risk weakening it.

A very practical reason also exists for defeating the prohibition amendment: it would be an administrative nightmare. For millions of Americans, drinking alcohol is both a long-standing cultural tradition and their private right. Enforcing a ban that millions of Americans do not support would create enormous problems for the federal government. Representative Fiorello La Guardia predicts that to enforce prohibition in New York City "will require a police force of 250,000 men and a force of 250,000 men to police the police." People from New York City and other major urban areas, especially in the Northeast, strongly oppose prohibition legislation.

Finally, if you make alcohol illegal, you invite organized crime to fill the high demand for it. The scarcity of liquor will cause prices to soar, and criminals will make huge fortunes on their product. People might smuggle in alcohol from other countries, and some individuals might set up secret stills and breweries. The government would have to spend an enormous amount of time, effort, and money to patrol thousands of miles of borders and shoreline and to uncover all of the illegal manufacturing of alcoholic beverages.

Option 2 Support the prohibition amendment.

You have a chance to create a revolutionary change in American society. Through your vote, you can help reduce crime, poverty, and other social ills. Billy Sunday, one of the nation's most influential preachers, declares in his famous "Booze Sermon" that by voting for prohibition, you will destroy the "parent of crimes and the mother of sins." Sunday charges that the alcohol industry is "the most damnable, corrupt institution that ever wriggled out of Hell and fastened itself on the public."

The benefits of this amendment seem almost endless. What the Anti-Saloon League claims is true: this law will give Americans the chance to live in a safe and healthy society. An end to the alcohol trade would immediately reduce the amount of crime in the country by eliminating the violent and irrational acts of drunken patrons. In addition, the amendment would keep irresponsible saloon operators from continuing their practice of serving alcohol to minors and promoting corruption and immorality in order to line their pockets with profits.

A former professional baseball player, Billy Sunday (1863-1935) was a popular evangelistic preacher in the early 1900s.

The prohibition amendment would solve many family problems by keeping parents sober and employed, by reducing the amount of abuse at the hands of a drunken family member, and by channeling wages that had been squandered on liquor into areas of genuine need. Moreover, the absence of alcohol would improve the health and life expectancy of many U.S. citizens.

Since the alcoholic beverages that you would be banning do not contribute anything positive to society, you can accomplish all these benefits virtually without cost. In fact, these changes would so reduce public expenditure on prisons, police, and services for the poor that the government could decrease taxes considerably.

To answer those who claim that such a ban is impractical, all you need to do is look at the states that already have prohibition laws. Those laws do not seem to be causing any problems. Kansas banned alcoholic beverages in 1881, and that ban appears to be working well. In fact, prohibitionists point out that the dry states are remarkably free of the kind of radical social unrest that is sweeping across many areas of the world. They claim that the use of alcohol leads to the social problems and disorder that leave nations vulnerable to rebellion. It was the disruptive effects of alcohol abuse, they say, that made Russia ripe for revolution.

Some critics say you cannot enforce a law that a large segment of society strongly opposes because millions will simply defy it. But the answer to that is simply to have strong and consistent enforcement. If the penalties are severe enough, and if you provide the funding for effective enforcement, people will not risk breaking the law.

If you need additional incentive for voting in favor of prohibition, consider patriotism. The United States is currently involved in a world war. The production of liquor and beer uses up a great deal of grain that could feed the U.S. troops in Europe. Thus, the greed of the alcohol industry is taking priority over the urgent needs of our armed forces. We should take steps to see that this does not continue.

Finally, prohibition is not a sudden, drastic action sprung on an unsuspecting alcoholic beverage industry. For decades, people have tried to get this industry to act responsibly. But the brewers and distillers, who own three-fourths of the saloons in the nation, have ignored all efforts to get them to reform or to compromise. Instead, they have funded a massive effort to fight prohibition. As long as wet states continue to allow alcoholic beverages, brewers in dry states can easily find ways around prohibition laws. The only way to solve the problem is to pass this amendment and create a national ban on alcohol—a ban that is supported by a majority of Americans.

Americans favoring prohibition—especially those living in the 24 southern, midwestern, and western states that have already passed prohibition legislation—have showered Congress with letters. And churches of every major Protestant denomination enthusiastically support prohibition. They consider the amendment the most important political issue of the day.

Option 3 Modify the amendment to ban only the sale, transportation, and importation of alcoholic beverages.

This compromise, which resembles the laws of many "dry" states, would eliminate many of the harmful effects of alcohol consumption. It would close down the saloons and cut down on public drunkenness. Yet it would not deprive citizens of their right to do as they choose in the privacy of their own homes.

The disadvantages of this compromise are that it would do little to prevent the kind of alcohol abuse that takes such a devastating toll on families. Also, it would encourage people to set up unsafe facilities for making alcohol in their homes. Furthermore, the enormous loopholes in the amendment would make enforcement of the

*For many city-dwellers, especially immigrants, the
corner pub was a place to socialize with friends, to
make business connections, and to talk politics.*

law difficult. People could set up large manufacturing
facilities and skirt the law by claiming that they were pro-
ducing alcohol for only their family and friends.

YOU ARE A SENATOR.
WHAT IS YOUR DECISION?

Option 1   **Oppose the prohibition amendment.**

Option 2   **Support the prohibition amendment.**

Option 3   **Modify the amendment to ban only
the sale, transportation, and
importation of alcoholic beverages.**

Senator Morris Sheppard (1875-1941), who would serve in the Senate until his death, called alcohol "one of the deadliest poisons known to man."

The Senate chose *Option 2*.

The Senate passed the prohibition amendment by a vote of 65 to 20 on August 1, 1917. Later that year, the measure passed in the House of Representatives. To become a law, a constitutional amendment also requires approval by three-fourths of the state legislatures. Within 13 months, 36 states had voted to adopt the amendment.

On January 16, 1919, the Eighteenth Amendment to the U.S. Constitution became law. The amendment granted a one-year transition before the ban on alcoholic beverages went into effect, so Prohibition actually began in 1920. The Volstead Act enforcing Prohibition—named for its sponsor, Minnesota representative Andrew Volstead—passed on October 28, 1919, over President Woodrow Wilson's veto.

Even though he sponsored the Volstead Act that gave the federal government the power to prosecute violations of the Eighteenth Amendment, Representative Andrew Volstead (1860-1947) was not a diehard prohibitionist.

Public Safety Director Smedley "Duckboards" Butler chops open barrels of beer and pours them into Philadelphia's Schuylkill River during Prohibition.

ANALYSIS

The "noble experiment," as many politicians called Prohibition, initially cut down on the consumption of alcohol. But after the initial decline, people began to spend more money on alcohol than they had before

Prohibition began. Because so many people were determined to drink despite the law, illegal activity overran much of the country. There were even 500 illegal liquor operations set up within sight of the White House!

This illegal activity overwhelmed the American justice system. From 1920 to 1930, federal prohibition agents arrested 577,000 people, seized 1.6 million illegal manufacturing operations, and killed hundreds of suspected prohibition violators. Most historians agree that these numbers represent only a small portion of the millions who violated Prohibition.

Congress initially set aside $2.2 million per year for the enforcement of the new law. But illegal activity grew so rapidly that the budget of the Bureau of Prohibition soared to $13.4 million per year during the 1920s. Every year, the U.S. Coast Guard spent an additional $13 million defending the coastline from illegal imports.

In 1929, the new prohibition commissioner estimated that he would need at least $300 million each year to enforce the law effectively. This did not include millions of dollars that state and local governments spent on the problem. Throughout the 1920s, Prohibition was a huge financial burden to the government, and it led to large increases in taxation and government spending.

Prohibition did not accomplish any of the goals that its supporters had promised. While prohibitionists had predicted that Americans would commit far fewer crimes, work harder, and support their families more responsibly, many social problems worsened. Furthermore, economic production did not improve; in fact, the United States plunged into its worst depression during Prohibition.

The Crusaders were one of many groups that formed to oppose the Eighteenth Amendment. Prohibition's opponents included many of the most powerful people in the nation—some of them former prohibitionists.

And organized crime connected with illegal liquor made the streets less safe. As the national homicide rate increased by 78 percent, major criminals such as Chicago's Al Capone became enormously wealthy.

Because the producers of illegal alcohol bribed officials, government also became more corrupt. Prohibition probably contributed to a huge increase in taxes over the pre-Prohibition rate because it eliminated a prime source of revenue—taxes on alcohol. Moreover, by forcing the production of liquor underground and away from government inspection, the amendment led to poisonous batches of liquor being sold. In fact, the government added poisons to the alcohol that was used in industrial production to keep people from drinking it. The *New York World* charged that "the United States government planned collective slaughter." In 1927 alone, nearly 12,000 Americans died from alcohol poisoning.

Within a few years, most Americans were ready to admit that Prohibition was a mistake. A 1926 poll conducted by the Newspaper Enterprise Association found that 81 percent of those who were surveyed wanted the law changed or eliminated altogether.

In late 1932, lawmakers set out to undo the damage they had done almost 15 years earlier. Senator John Blaine from Wisconsin introduced the Twenty-First Amendment, which called for a repeal of the Eighteenth Amendment. Congress passed the amendment, and three-fourths of the states had ratified the repeal within a year. The country's great experiment came to an end when the nation repealed a constitutional amendment for the only time in U.S. history.

*Patrons celebrate the end of Prohibition at a saloon in
St. Paul, Minnesota, in 1933.*

Although prohibition is currently a dead issue in
the United States, a similar debate continues over the
effectiveness of laws banning the sale and use of drugs
such as marijuana. Supporters say these laws are necessary
to maintain social order, but opponents cite the
Prohibition experience as evidence that laws controlling
personal use are unproductive and impossible to enforce.

2

SOCIAL SECURITY
August 1935

The United States is struggling to pull out of a devastating economic depression. Many people have lost their jobs, their homes, and their life's savings. During 1932 alone, a quarter of a million Americans lost their homes because they could not make their mortgage payments. The most heartbreaking of these losses hit the elderly. Many of them have either used up or lost their savings and are no longer able to work. In response to this crisis, the Senate is considering a proposal to create a national social security program to provide a guaranteed income for elderly people after their retirement.

The federal government has already stepped in and provided emergency relief. By autumn 1934, the government was disbursing financial assistance for food and shelter to almost 18.5 million impoverished Americans. This assistance, which cost $500 million in 1933, has put an enormous strain on the federal government, but has provided no long-term solution to the problems of the destitute elderly.

The proposed social security program would deduct a certain amount of money from a worker's paycheck and would require the employer to make an equivalent contribution. This money would be put into a fund. Then when the worker reached retirement age, he or she would receive a monthly payment based on the amount of money contributed to the fund during his or her working years.

Many elderly people lost their life savings when bank failures spread across the country during the first few years of the Great Depression, which began in 1929.

Charities and other relief organizations provided free meals during the Depression's worst years, when about one of every four workers was unemployed.

BACKGROUND

Recently, Senator Huey Long of Louisiana and a doctor named Francis Townsend from California have each called for some radical measures to address these issues, and their plans are gaining a groundswell of public support. Senator Long's Share Our Wealth Society proposes that the government seize some income and assets from the wealthiest Americans for redistribution to those in need. Townsend recommends a general sales tax to provide old-age pensions for all elderly people, whether or not they need it. The popularity of these extreme proposals has made it necessary to find an alternative answer to the problems they are attempting to solve.

Senator Huey Long's plan to redistribute wealth, which promised a guaranteed family income and housing allowance, was cut short when he was assassinated in September 1935.

In an effort to find a lasting solution to the suffering of the elderly, as well as to unemployment and the lack of health insurance, Democratic president Franklin Roosevelt created a Committee on Economic Security to come up with possible plans. On January 15, 1935, the committee issued a report urging the United States to adopt a national social security system patterned after the system that Germany had pioneered in the late nineteenth century. The system would provide a guaranteed monthly payment for all citizens once they reached the age of 65. Senator Robert Wagner, a Democrat from New York, has now proposed this legislation.

Because President Roosevelt wants to avoid another relief program, he insists that funds for the social security system come from deductions the government takes out of workers' paychecks, which would be matched by employer contributions. He also requires that the amount the government pays to recipients be based on the total they contribute during their working lives.

Roosevelt believes these two requirements would help both workers and lawmakers see the deductions as retirement contributions to which workers are entitled, rather than just another tax. Thus, no future government would be able to abandon the system and refuse to pay the workers because both the recipients and the government would see the money as the workers' by right.

In effect, the plan before Congress is a forced retirement savings program. The government will put workers' contributions into a fund. The regular contribution of the workers and the buildup of interest revenue will increase the fund's value over the years. By the time each generation of workers retires, the amount they contributed, plus the accrued interest, will be large enough to provide for basic needs for the rest of their lives.

THE DECISION IS YOURS.

How will you vote on the proposal to have the government create a national social security program?

Option 1 Support the social security proposal.

A social security program makes sense in a modern society for the simple reason that it provides peace of mind for elderly persons. After years of work, people deserve a rest. And as they age and lose their physical ability to perform their jobs as well as they did when they were younger, they deserve a chance to retire. Once people retire, they no longer earn an income, and their only support for the rest of their lives is the money they saved during their working years. Some people, however, do not have the self-discipline to save for retirement. This social security proposal would force them to contribute regularly to their own retirement fund.

But social security is far more than a bailout program for those who would otherwise squander their money during their youth or plan poorly for their later years. As the average life span of Americans increases, many people are living well past the age of retirement. Given this increase in life expectancy, those with modest incomes face a difficult decision. Should they deprive themselves of a better standard of living now to save for their later years? If they die soon after retirement, they will have sacrificed all those years for nothing. Or, what about those people who live to be 100 years old and have no support for the last years of their lives? And what if retired people who have been saving responsibly for many years suddenly have their savings wiped out by an accident or a severe illness or by the bank failures that are now sweeping the country? Where will they find the income they unexpectedly need?

Social security will take the guesswork out of retirement. If enough people contribute enough money to provide for 10 to 15 years of retirement, everyone will be able to draw from that pool in the years between their

retirement and their death because the early deaths and
the long lives will average out.

In the long run, this plan will be more constructive
and humane than the current system in which the government bails out those people who have no money. Such
a system of welfare helps no one because it requires tax-
payers to support a never-ending line of destitute people
and eats away at the pride of those who can survive only
by relying on the charity of others. As President
Roosevelt says, "Continued dependence upon relief
induces a spiritual and moral disintegration fundamentally
destructive to the national fiber. . . . The federal government must and shall quit this business of relief."

The social security system, on the other hand,
removes the embarrassment of welfare. Retired workers
can feel entitled to their monthly social security checks
because they earned them through their payroll contributions earlier in their lives. The system is hardly radical
or untried. Ever since Chancellor Otto von Bismarck
introduced social security in Germany in the 1880s, the
system has worked effectively there and in other
European nations as well.

The committee that recommended this plan to the
U.S. government included top professionals from many
fields, including labor, agriculture, business, religion, government, and social work. To deal with the problems of
the elderly, these professionals agreed on a plan that cre-
ates a vast pool of wealth without imposing any major
hardships on business or individuals.

The government has an obligation to see that all of
its citizens enjoy a respectable standard of living. You

can either adopt this system or continue to pour money into services for the growing number of impoverished.

Option 2 Oppose the social security proposal.

The last thing that the United States needs is for the federal government to get into the business of managing people's money. The government has never shown itself to be an efficient money manager. Quite the contrary, says Republican governor Alf Landon of Kansas, who believes that the social security system would produce a gigantic bureaucratic mess. He argues that the plan would allow the big spenders in Washington to raise and

As the Republican presidential candidate in 1936, Governor Alf Landon (1887-1987), carried only the states of Vermont and Maine against the popular incumbent, President Franklin Roosevelt.

waste billions of dollars. Such diverse groups as the American Federation of Labor and the U.S. Chamber of Commerce, as well as the *New York Times*, agree with him.

Supreme Court Justice Louis Brandeis, who possesses one of the finest legal minds in the country, argues that the U.S. Senate is not the place to experiment with a social security program. Instead, Brandeis believes that social experiments are better handled by the states.

Republican senator Arthur Vandenberg of Michigan does not like the idea of creating a huge reserve of money to pay out future benefits because he does not trust the federal government to keep its hands off that reserve. What if the government ends up spending the social security contributions on other government programs?

Economists also voice objections to the plan, but for different reasons. President Roosevelt may call the amount deducted from a worker's check a "contribution," but the payroll deduction has the same effect as a tax. The deduction takes money away from workers and employers and gives it to the government for a long period of time. When consumers do not have money to spend on products or services, the economy suffers, and such a tax increase would take even more money out of consumers' hands. The economy is currently so weak that it would be a bad idea to deduct more money from the workers' paychecks. Furthermore, this plan will add another burdensome tax on businesses when they are struggling to survive in the midst of the Depression.

The government can offset the effects of a tax increase on a weak economy by spending money on goods and services. But with social security, the government would simply be holding the money for the future without putting any of it to immediate use. In other words, the government would raise taxes considerably without using any of the money to pay for benefits. It would then have to raise taxes again to pay for other government programs that might be needed in years to come. Will American citizens, who are already feeling the pinch of increased taxes, rebel at the prospect of even more taxes?

Also, the social security program might encourage citizens to become careless about their personal savings and retirement plans. Social security is meant to provide only a very basic level of income in order to keep people from extreme poverty. Workers, however, might begin to rely too much on social security to provide for their retirement. If that happens, workers might save less on their own. In turn, their failure to save might offset the social security contributions that came out of their paychecks. A reduced amount of private savings would be another dangerous blow to a weak economy.

Finally, the social security program could cause unwanted changes in society because it sets the retirement age for receiving benefits at 65. The law would encourage people to retire at age 65, even though some could continue to work productively beyond that age.

Option 3 Work for a modified form of social security.

You agree that a social security plan is needed, but you think there is a better way to fund it. Instead of paying out social security benefits from a large reserve pool, what if the government decided to use this year's contributions from younger workers to pay benefits for this year's recipients? There would then be no huge reserve of money that the government might be tempted to spend. This is known as the "pay-as-you-go" plan.

The argument against this plan is that social security ends up being an extra tax for government programs, funded by the workers who can least afford to pay more taxes. Because life expectancy is increasing and the birth rate is decreasing, there will be fewer workers supporting more elderly in future years. Therefore, as more people retire and the claims for benefits go up, you would also have to schedule future tax increases.

A more drastic change would be to get the government out of the retirement savings business altogether. Private business is better equipped to handle people's money because the competitive nature of business makes it more efficient and open to people's needs. Why not simply require everyone to participate in some kind of private retirement plan? Why not deduct the money from people's paychecks and put it into one of these retirement plans instead of giving it to the government?

YOU ARE A SENATOR.
WHAT IS YOUR DECISION?

Option 1　　**Support the social security proposal.**

Option 2　　**Oppose the social security proposal.**

Option 3　　**Work for a modified form of social security.**

One of the major proponents of President Roosevelt's New Deal legislation, Senator Robert Wagner (1877-1953) fought for the protection of workers and for affordable housing.

The Senate chose *Option 1*.

On August 9, 1935, the Senate approved the Social
Security Act, one day after the House of Representatives
had voted for it. President Roosevelt signed the bill into
law on August 14, 1935. The act established a system of
payroll deductions for many wage earners (***Option 1***). As
the original law required, savings were invested in a
reserve account in the form of U.S. Treasury bonds, to be
paid to contributors when they reached the age of 65.

*Senator Robert Wagner (standing third from left) and
other government officials, including Secretary of Labor
Frances Perkins (in hat), watch as President Franklin
Roosevelt signs the Social Security Act of 1935.*

Within a few years, however, Congress changed the law so that current Social Security benefits were paid from current Social Security taxes (*Option 3*).

The payroll tax began in 1937, the year the federal courts declared the law to be acceptable under the U.S. Constitution. The government began paying out Social Security benefits in 1942.

ANALYSIS

The American people overwhelmingly accepted the basic idea of Social Security: a guaranteed income for the elderly. According to the authors of *Launching Social Security*, "The Social Security Act marked a belated acceptance of the general principle of social insurance which western European nations had developed at least a generation earlier."

During the first 40 years of the Social Security program, few lawmakers challenged the concept. Today, the program has such deep roots that some critics refer to it as a "sacred cow" of American politics—a program having such strong public support that no one would dare touch the system, regardless of how much harm it causes.

The Social Security Act has accomplished what the lawmakers intended. It has provided basic financial support for the elderly in retirement. The act has thus kept millions of people from extended poverty or from having to depend on charity and public relief. Social Security checks currently provide the largest source of income for roughly one-third of elderly Americans and a substantial portion of income for another third.

These benefits, however, have not come without cost. In recent years, the Social Security program has begun to run into some major problems. As Americans live longer, a larger percentage have become eligible for benefits while a smaller percentage contribute to the program. In 1950, for example, only one in eight Americans who reached the age of 65 could expect to survive until the age of 90. Now that figure is one in four.

When prices rise and economic production in the United States decreases, the gap between what workers and employers contribute to Social Security and the amount the government is obligated to pay out widens. In order to collect enough money to provide benefits, the government has raised the Social Security contribution dramatically. While the original Social Security Act called for a paycheck deduction of 1 percent of a worker's pay and an equal contribution from the employer, the tax now stands at more than 15 percent, half of which is paid by the employee and half by the employer.

The problem will certainly get worse. Because the birthrate in the United States has slowed, the proportion of young people is less than it was in the past. As the large "baby boom" generation of the 1950s retires, the burden of providing Social Security for them will fall on a much smaller group of younger workers. In other words, more people will be entitled to benefits while fewer people will be contributing to the fund.

This problem looms so large that most middle-aged and younger workers have lost confidence in the Social Security system. Even though they will have contributed thousands of dollars to the fund during their working

As Senator Arthur Vandenberg (1884-1951) had warned in 1935, the federal government now uses the surplus in social security to offset the federal deficit instead of saving it for future recipients.

lives, most of them doubt that any benefits will be available for them when they retire.

Furthermore, the 1935 fear of some senators that the government would be tempted to use Social Security money for other purposes has proven to be well founded. Currently, the federal government uses billions of dollars of Social Security revenue to help make up for the fact that it spends more money than it takes in.

Finally, the Social Security system is so costly that it leaves little money for other programs. Currently, the federal government spends more than 10 times as much on the elderly as it does on children. Critics question the wisdom and fairness of a system that funnels the federal government's funds to the elderly, many of whom are financially well-off, at the expense of young people, who are often struggling to make ends meet.

3

LABOR STRIKES
June 1947

Labor unions are striking all across the United States and shutting down an alarming number of factories and industries. Many Americans believe this is a result of the growing power that labor unions have amassed over the years, much of it because of laws passed by the United States Congress.

In response to this problem, the Senate is considering the Labor-Management Relations bill of 1947. More commonly known as the Taft-Hartley bill, the proposal is named for the two Republican members of Congress who introduced it, Senator Robert A. Taft of Ohio and Representative Fred Hartley of New Jersey. The Taft-Hartley bill would guarantee rights for employers and nonunion workers while cutting back on the power of labor unions. For example, it would ban the common

More restrictive than Senator Taft's, Representative Fred Hartley's version of the Labor-Management Relations bill banned mass picketing by workers and prohibited unions from organizing employees industry wide for bargaining purposes.

union practice of the "closed shop," which forces employers to hire only those workers who belong to a union.

BACKGROUND

Labor unions grew out of the Industrial Revolution of the nineteenth century. Employers learned methods of mass production that prompted them to hire thousands of workers. These workers toiled in appalling conditions, poor and powerless, while employers often became rich and had total control over their businesses. Moreover, as hundreds of thousands of immigrants poured into the United States, employers could easily replace a difficult worker with any of the thousands of other people who were seeking employment. Because they had no power to negotiate, workers had to take the wages that employers offered or look for another job.

Labor unions allowed workers to negotiate for better working conditions. Because employers lost power over their employees when the workers banded together, many companies did all they could to crush the unions. But then the U.S. government stepped in and passed laws that recognized the right of workers to organize unions.

One of the most popular and effective union organizers in the United States for 50 years, Mary Harris "Mother" Jones (1830-1930) helped to found the Industrial Workers of the World in 1905.

During the first quarter of the twentieth century, union membership soared. In 1897, only 1.5 percent of the labor force belonged to unions. By 1920, that number had grown to 18.4 percent.

The prosperity of the 1920s actually hurt the union movement as high-paying jobs made unions seem less necessary. In addition, the courts restricted some unionizing activities. Then the Great Depression, which began in 1929, further weakened unions. Businesses suffered so badly that companies laid off many employees. Jobs became so scarce that workers had to accept any job that was available, no matter how long the hours or low the pay. Once again, employers had the upper hand.

President Franklin D. Roosevelt sought to protect workers' rights in the National Industrial Recovery Act, which required that employees play a role in making decisions in the workplace. Employers set up company unions in response. Company unions, loyal to management, replaced unions that had worked for the interests of labor. By 1934, total union membership in the United States dropped to less than 12 percent of the work force—and many of these workers were members of company unions.

To protect workers, Congress passed the National Labor Relations Act (often called the Wagner Act) in 1935. Guaranteeing the right to unionize, the act banned such practices as the organization of company unions, and it set up a National Labor Review Board to hear complaints about unfair management practices.

As unions gained more power, union membership again rose. By 1940, union membership made up more than 25 percent of the nonfarm work force. Then, when

Many felt the Wagner Act of 1935 had made unions too powerful and had led to violence and destruction such as this 1937 strike against the American Gas Machine Company in Minnesota.

the United States entered World War II, government and industry went all-out to produce materials that would help the war effort. During the war years, the government froze wages and prices and prohibited strikes.

When the war ended in 1945, the government lifted these controls. Businesses hiked their prices and again started to rake in great profits. Labor unions, which had risen in membership to more than 35 percent of the non-farm work force, demanded their share of the new wealth. When employers did not give the unions what they wanted, workers went out on strike.

Major industries, such as automobile and steel manufacturing and meatpacking, were the first to shut down.

More workers went on strike together than at any other point in history. By January 1946, a full three percent of the work force was on strike. Late in that same year, lost worker-days (the number of workers times the number of days they work) grew to between 3 and 6 million per month because of strikes.

Industry seems helpless to settle the rash of strikes. If these work stoppages continue, Americans' standard of living will drop. This fear has led to a widespread feeling among Americans that the balance of power has now tilted too heavily in favor of unions. Supported by popular opinion, industry leaders have urged Congress to pass legislation that will restore a more reasonable balance of power between employers and unions.

THE DECISION IS YOURS.

How will you vote on the Taft-Hartley bill, which strengthens employers' rights in dealing with labor unions?

Option 1 Support the Taft-Hartley bill.

The bill is nothing more than an attempt to restore a proper balance of power between labor and management. Most of its provisions simply try to establish fair play by allowing employers to manage their own businesses. Currently, the laws are so heavily weighted in favor of unions that an employer does not have a fair chance to conduct a successful operation.

Among the many reasonable provisions of the Taft-Hartley bill are the following:

1. Employers can express opinions about unions and union activities as long as they don't threaten their employees. (Currently, employers are not supposed to say anything to discourage union organizing. This denies employers the right to freedom of speech—a right the Constitution guarantees to all Americans.)

2. Employers can call for union elections. (This would help employers discover whether union leadership really represents the workers.)

3. Closed shops in which unions demand that employers hire only workers who are members of the union are outlawed. (This protects the rights of employers to decide whom they will hire.)

4. States have the right to outlaw union shops in which all employees at a business site must join the union after being hired. (Unions should respect the rights of individuals who do not want to join a union and should not require that the employer deduct union dues from a worker's paycheck without the worker's permission.)

5. Unions must bargain in good faith with employers. (As a matter of fair play, both unions and employers must try to find solutions to labor problems.)

6. Unfair labor practices, such as secondary boycotts, are prohibited. (In a secondary boycott, workers who are not directly involved in a dispute go on strike to support workers who are already striking against another employer. When workers stage secondary boycotts, employers face strikes that have nothing to do with their own employment practices.)

7. Management has the right to sue the union for any damages caused by union activities, including strike

violence. (Again, this gives employers the same constitutional rights as all American citizens.)

8. Unions must give management a 60-day notice of their intent to strike, and unions are prohibited from striking before the end of their contracts. (These provisions give workers and management time to work out a reasonable solution to their disputes.)

9. The president of the United States has the right to order a union to stop a strike if the strike puts the health or safety of the nation in danger.

10. Communists are prohibited from holding any union posts. (Most Americans at this time believe Communists advocate ideas that threaten the very existence of the United States.)

Most Republicans and a majority of voters in the South, Midwest, and West believe these are reasonable and necessary steps that will correct some of the imbalance in the relations between employers and workers and will prevent unions from abusing their power. If the Senate adopts the Taft-Hartley bill, management and unions will probably work together to solve their disputes rather than engage in tests of strength that could paralyze the nation with strikes.

Option 2 Oppose the Taft-Hartley bill.

Most people who have any sympathy for the common worker are outraged at many of the provisions of this bill. Labor leaders call it the "Tuff-Heartless Act" and the "Slave Labor Act." One labor leader declares that it is a "deliberate and monstrous movement . . . to cripple if not destroy the labor movement." Democratic president

President Harry S. Truman had called for legislation to control some of the activity of labor unions, but he believed that the Taft-Hartley bill went too far.

Harry S. Truman argues that "industrial peace cannot be achieved merely by laws directed against labor unions." He believes the Taft-Hartley bill will create more problems than it will solve. Most Democratic senators agree.

The Taft-Hartley bill clearly discriminates against unions and takes the side of management. History has shown the danger of the government abandoning its protection of unions. Without strong unions, workers would be as powerless as they were in the past.

If this bill were enacted into law, employers would once again use their wealth and influence to get government officials to do whatever the employers want. Moreover, many judges (who are often people with wealth and influence) would support employers in court cases. In the early days of union activity, judges repeatedly sided with big business leaders in their decisions and showed no sympathy for the plight of the common worker. Without federal government protection firmly in place, this situation would return.

Attempts to outlaw union shops and closed shops would destroy the labor movement. Workers will have a voice in working conditions only if they stick together. Because all workers benefit from the bargaining power of their unions, they should all be obligated to contribute to their unions' efforts. Once management breaks up the unions, the workers will again be powerless.

Basically, this bill is an overreaction to the situation of widespread strikes. If the members of Congress take time to think about the issue, they will realize the current rash of strikes is a temporary result of inflationary economic conditions brought on by the war. That situation will not last. Employers and workers will again negotiate to find acceptable solutions to their disputes.

The worst problem with Taft-Hartley is that it brings big government into industry to dictate solutions. By introducing a web of new government regulations into labor issues, you would create a bureaucratic nightmare. The government does not need to meddle in problems that management and labor negotiators can solve better by themselves. Some analysts say that the bill would do little for either the unions or the employers. The only people who would really benefit from the passage of this act are lawyers because employers and unions would have to call on them to interpret the legal messes that this legislation would create.

One example of a possible problem is the provision banning Communists from holding union posts. Because such a provision would violate many union constitutions, unions would have to rewrite their charters and then vote on them. That action would make all of the contracts already in force between companies and the unions under the old charters invalid. How would the courts decide which contracts to enforce?

Senator Robert Taft, who is sponsoring the bill in order to curb what he sees as an unfair labor advantage, seems to recognize this danger. Taft has said, "Walkouts are not as serious as represented in newspaper headlines, and it is far better . . . to suffer the inconvenience of strikes than have a completely government regulated economy." Although Taft's version of the bill is much more moderate than Hartley's, it still advocates significant government intrusion. By promoting this kind of government regulation, Taft is acting like a hypocrite.

Finally, the government would have a difficult time enforcing many provisions of the law. Labor unions are furious over some of the bill's provisions, and they are so powerful in many areas of the country, especially the industrial states of the Northeast, that local government officials will not dare challenge them.

*Minnesota senator Joseph Ball led a faction of
20 to 30 senators who demanded tougher anti-
union measures, including a ban on union shops.*

Option 3 Work for a stronger law.

Many business leaders and Republican senators
believe that the Taft-Hartley bill is not hard enough on
labor. Labor unions have already destroyed employers'
right to run their businesses the way they see fit. A business is a personal enterprise and the owner's livelihood is
at stake. If the business fails, labor unions are not going to
lift a finger to help the employer.

Given this situation, why should an employer be forced to hire employees under conditions demanded by the workers? After all, no one forces a worker to work for an employer. The worker can decide whether or not a particular working situation is to his or her liking and then choose to work there or to seek work elsewhere.

The government has already given too many advantages to the worker. The nationwide strikes are a result of unions using these advantages to make impossible demands. Unions have gotten so powerful and arrogant that they are threatening to destroy America's economic well-being.

Therefore, you need a stronger bill than the Taft-Hartley bill. You should hold out for a bill that would give the employer the right to set conditions as he or she sees fit. Now, when the American public is most irritated by the power of labor unions, is the time to enact such a bill.

YOU ARE A SENATOR.
WHAT IS YOUR DECISION?

Option 1   **Support the Taft-Hartley bill.**

Option 2   **Oppose the Taft-Hartley bill.**

Option 3   **Work for a stronger law.**

Senator Robert Taft (1889-1953), the son of former president William Howard Taft, was often called "Mr. Republican" because he was such a recognized leader of conservative Republicans.

The Senate chose *Option 1*.

After the House of Representatives passed its version of the bill, the Senate passed the Taft-Hartley measure by a vote of 68 to 24. President Truman vetoed the bill, but the House of Representatives voted to override his veto. On June 23, 1947, the Senate likewise overrode the president's veto, 68 to 25, and the bill became law.

ANALYSIS

The Taft-Hartley Act was one of the most controversial laws ever passed by the U.S. Congress. Its first result was to aggravate the problem of strikes—more than 200,000 coal miners immediately walked off their jobs to protest the new law.

Many of the predictions made by the law's opponents came true, and the most powerful unions found ways to get around some provisions of the law. For example, the government made no serious attempt to enforce the ban on closed shops because the closed-shop tradition was so powerful on the loading docks and in the building trades. Unions got around the restrictions on striking before the end of a contract period by getting management to waive those restrictions.

The law did not weaken the labor movement as much as many of its supporters had hoped. Management had suspected that many workers supported unions only because of union intimidation. But when employers demanded secret-ballot union elections, as the new law allowed, they found unions were more popular than they

Even though the Taft-Hartley Act limited the power of labor unions, union members, such as these retail workers striking in St. Paul, Minnesota, in 1949, continued to organize to gain better working conditions.

had thought. In the decade following the adoption of the Taft-Hartley Act, unions won 98 percent of the secret-ballot votes over whether to set up union shops. Union membership actually increased by about 3 million in the decade following Taft-Hartley.

Today, labor relations analysts believe that many of the problems the legislation was meant to solve would have faded away on their own without the bill. During the prosperous 1950s, labor and management learned how to cooperate better. As manufacturers replaced more

Organized labor gained strength with the 1955 merger of the two most powerful union organizations, the American Federation of Labor (AFL) and the Congress of Industrial Organizations (CIO). Former AFL president George Meany (center) became the AFL-CIO's first president.

and more workers with automation in the 1960s, and as many unskilled jobs moved to low-wage foreign nations, union influence began to shrink. These trends, more than the Taft-Hartley Act, accounted for the fact that by the 1990s the percentage of union members in the labor force had dropped to half of what it was in the 1940s. And strikes in 1992 cost the United States almost 97 percent fewer lost work days than they had in the 1940s.

Nevertheless, the Taft-Hartley Act was an important piece of legislation. By curbing some of the growing power of unions and recognizing the legal rights of employers, it had helped to restore a balance in labor relations.

Equally important, the act did not take drastic action against unions. With widespread strikes fueling resentment and fear, many business leaders and politicians believed this was the time to bring the unions to their knees. Senator Taft crafted his bill to defuse some of their hostilities and counteract some of the more extreme measures proposed against unions. As a result, the law was able to achieve many of its goals without the storm of civil unrest that might have accompanied stronger anti-union measures.

4

PUBLIC DISCRIMINATION
June 1964

The Senate is considering the strongest civil rights bill in its history—a bill that would grant equal opportunities to all United States citizens regardless of race, color, religion, or national origin. In particular, sponsors of the legislation hope to end centuries of public discrimination against African Americans.

Among the main provisions of the 1964 bill are the following:

1. Enforce the constitutional right of all adult citizens to vote in federal elections.

2. Ban discrimination in businesses that provide services to the public, such as hotels, restaurants, and movie theaters.

3. Ban discrimination in business practices of hiring and giving promotions.

4. Ban discrimination in all programs supported by federal funds.

5. Desegregate all public schools and colleges.

BACKGROUND

When European settlers brought African slaves to the American colonies more than three centuries ago, they created a racial problem that has plagued the continent ever since. The founders of the United States waffled on the issue of slavery. While revolutionary spirit inspired many northern states to outlaw slavery, the U.S. Constitution did not recognize black slaves as citizens, and the country continued to allow slavery in many states until the end of the Civil War.

In 1863, President Abraham Lincoln took one step toward granting equal rights to African Americans by issuing the Emancipation Proclamation. That act freed the slaves in the southern states that had seceded from the rest of the nation. Following the end of the war in 1865, the U.S. Congress banned slavery outright and passed the Fourteenth Amendment to guarantee equal rights for all American citizens.

The amendment stated:

> No State shall make or enforce any law which shall abridge the privileges or immunities of citizens of the United States; nor shall any State deprive any person of life, liberty, or property, without due process of law; nor deny to any person within its jurisdiction the equal protection of the laws.

This amendment, however, did not achieve what its supporters had intended. Many state governments passed laws that discriminated against black citizens. In southern states, statutes called *Jim Crow* laws made it illegal for blacks to use white facilities. The public bathrooms, schools, and kinds of transportation that were designated for blacks were minimal and inferior. In 1896, the Supreme Court of the United States upheld the southern claim that such facilities were "separate but equal"—even though they were clearly not equal.

Some states also used the "separate-but-equal" concept to deny blacks their legal and economic rights. Whites owning private businesses refused to serve black customers. In addition, state governments enacted voting taxes, literacy tests, and other requirements to deny blacks the right to vote in elections. For decades, the U.S. Congress offered no encouragement or aid to blacks in their struggle for equal rights.

In 1954, the U.S. Supreme Court struck down the principle of separate-but-equal facilities and ordered state governments to begin integrating their public schools. After the early protests of the civil rights movement had begun, Congress passed watered-down civil rights bills in 1957 and 1960, but these laws were weak and ineffective.

Led by people such as Martin Luther King Jr. and James Farmer, blacks began to speak out in an effort to focus national attention on the injustices against them. Their protests have convinced a majority of Americans that blacks deserve better treatment under the law.

But some whites have struck back viciously against civil rights organizers, and some blacks have grown more

In 1955, Martin Luther King Jr. (second from right in foreground) led a boycott of the Montgomery, Alabama, buses to protest segregated seating. For more than a year, 50,000 blacks walked to work until the U.S. Supreme Court ruled the seating policy unconstitutional, ending the boycott.

outspoken in an effort to secure equal rights for their people. Much of the country is now in turmoil as demonstrations sweep through the inner cities.

President John F. Kennedy, a Democrat, proposed strong civil rights legislation to combat the injustices suffered by African Americans. But before Congress could take action on his proposals, Kennedy was assassinated. Vice-President Lyndon Johnson, a Texan, took over the presidency and vowed to carry on Kennedy's program.

After a long and emotional debate, the House passed the Civil Rights bill on February 10, 1964, by a vote of 290 to 130 and sent it to the Senate. The Senate bill was introduced by Democratic senators Mike Mansfield of Montana and Hubert H. Humphrey of Minnesota.

On August 28, 1963, about 200,000 people who were gathered for the March on Washington heard Martin Luther King Jr. declare "I Have a Dream"—for peace, justice, and equality.

THE DECISION IS YOURS.

How will you vote on the civil rights legislation that has come before the Senate?

Option 1 Support the civil rights bill.

Racial discrimination is wrong because it allows one group of Americans to treat another group as if they were inferior. Discrimination humiliates and impoverishes the minority group. By allowing such discriminatory policies to stay in place for so many years, the United States Senate has turned its back on the principle of equality for all.

The United States takes pride in being the land of liberty, a place where every individual has rights that the government cannot deny. So how can it continue to deny basic freedoms to a large percentage of its population? The late President Kennedy proclaimed that this civil rights bill is about nothing less than "common sense and common justice." And as President Johnson declares, "A hundred years ago Lincoln signed the Emancipation Proclamation, but until education is unaware of race, until employment is blind to color, emancipation will be a proclamation, but it will not be a fact."

The United States must live up to its promise of equality. As a United States senator, you have promised to defend the nation's laws and the U.S. Constitution. If you refuse to pass legislation that supports the principles of equality as stated in the Fourteenth Amendment, you are violating that pledge. The proposed legislation does not give black people any special privileges. It seeks only to give them a fair chance for decent jobs, decent education, and, most of all, decent lives.

Supporters such as Democratic representative Robert Kastenmeier of Wisconsin argue that now is the best time to enact such a law. Martin Luther King Jr. has brought the issue to the forefront, and his peaceful tactics have given it a moral force that many Americans and most Democrats find convincing. Many Republicans also support strong civil rights legislation. In fact, the efforts of Republican representative Bill McCulloch of Ohio ensured the bill's passage in the House of Representatives. Republican former president Dwight D. Eisenhower reminds Republicans that they are the party of Abraham Lincoln and therefore "have a particular obligation to be vigorous in the furtherance of civil rights."

In 1957, President Dwight D. Eisenhower (center), meeting here with civil rights leaders, ordered federal troops to help desegregate public schools in Little Rock, Arkansas.

The Senate should act now before extremists on both sides create a storm of hostility, resentment, and suspicion that will pit Americans against each other. By acting decisively, the Senate could heal some of the racial divisions that have festered far too long in this country. Either lawmakers help solve the problem rationally, fairly, and courageously now, or they will stand by helplessly while the situation explodes into outright racial warfare.

The opponents of the bill maintain that it gives the federal government the right to seize powers that belong to state governments. But they are wrong! The federal government has an obligation to see that every state in the union obeys the Constitution. This law is simply an attempt to enforce the constitutional guarantee of equal treatment for all citizens.

Opponents also say that this bill takes away the rights of private citizens. It forces them to provide services that they do not want to provide and dictates how they must run their own businesses. But there is nothing new or unconstitutional in this type of law. As Senator Humphrey states, laws say bar owners cannot serve liquor to children, and they also set sanitary standards for restaurants. Eating establishments must follow these laws to stay in business. Yet no one complains that regulations such as these violate the right of citizens to run their private businesses as they see fit.

The provision of the civil rights bill that forbids discrimination against customers is no different from these other laws. Whenever private choice harms the public well-being, the government has a right to set regulations to protect society.

For all the fuss that opponents to the bill have made, the act itself proposes nothing that is either radical or even innovative. Undoubtedly, the proposed law will work, since, as Senator Humphrey points out, the guarantee of equal access to public accommodation in the bill would simply "declare as a national policy what already exists in 32 states." And the public supports the civil rights bill by nearly a two-to-one margin.

Option 2 Oppose the civil rights bill.

While only a small percentage of the people would argue in favor of denying black people their constitutional rights, this bill is not the way to go about solving America's racial problems. Just because a law addresses a problem does not mean the law is good. For example, crime in the United States could be reduced by locking up all convicted criminals for life. But that does not mean the solution is a good one. You must defeat this bill because it is a bad way to achieve a good end. White southerners are particularly incensed by this legislation.

The main problem with this bill is that it gives the federal government a wide range of powers that the U.S. Constitution delegated to the states. The writers of the Constitution were suspicious of government, especially of a strong central government that was far removed from the wishes of the people.

To limit the damage that the federal government could do, the framers of the Constitution divided the powers of government among different branches and between the state and federal governments. This way, no one governmental body would ever attain so much power that it could control the lives of U.S. citizens. The Constitution delegates any powers not specifically granted to the federal government—including the powers in this bill—to the states.

That extension of federal power makes this a very dangerous bill. Representative Ed Willis, a Democrat from Louisiana, calls this proposal "the most drastic and far-reaching grab for power in history." One of the worst things about this bill is that it grants the U.S. attorney general great powers of law enforcement against the states. Senator Barry Goldwater, a Republican from Arizona, believes that this civil rights act will result in "the creation of a federal police force of mammoth proportions." He envisions a nightmare in which the federal government becomes a virtual dictatorship, recruiting neighbors to spy on each other to sniff out violations of the long list of federal civil rights regulations.

Democratic senator Strom Thurmond of South Carolina observes that eight years after Congress passed a similar bill in 1875, the Supreme Court declared it unconstitutional because it invaded people's rights to privacy and control over their own property. Why waste time on a bill that the courts will declare unconstitutional?

The bill is also flawed because it does not clearly define discrimination. In fact, it gives the federal courts and the attorney general's office broad powers to decide whether or not someone has broken the law. If the law cannot clearly define what discrimination is and what it is not, the senators should not put the law on the books.

The worst provisions in the bill, however, are those that ban discrimination in hiring and in businesses that

After years as a Democrat and "States' Rights Democrat"— including a 1948 third-party presidential run— Strom Thurmond became a Republican in 1964 in reaction to the Democratic Party's strong support of civil rights.

provide services to the public—such as hotels, restaurants, and theaters. In *U.S. News & World Report*, David Lawrence warned, "The present 'civil rights' bill . . . would bestow upon the courts the power to compel anyone engaged in business to give up his privacy—the right to hire the employees of his choice or to serve whatever customers he wishes."

When people engage in business, they should have the freedom to run their companies as they see fit. If you deny them this freedom, you are forcing them to do something they do not want to do. In other words, you are imposing a form of slavery on them. Is that what a civil rights bill should be doing?

The point is not whether you think discriminating against customers or job applicants is right, but that the federal government has no business dictating whom a business owner should hire or serve. You cannot expect the federal government to solve every problem, and this is one of those problems that is beyond its scope.

Furthermore, you cannot change people's attitudes by passing laws. The only way you can truly end discrimination in the United States is by persuading people that discrimination is wrong. The people who most strongly oppose this legislation are white southern voters. If you represent a southern state, you will certainly lose any chance for reelection if you vote for this bill.

Option 3 Work for a compromise bill.

While most Americans support some sort of civil rights legislation, many whites feel that things are going too far, too fast. Typical of this attitude is that of an Oklahoma City banker who agrees that blacks "have been mistreated and should have increased opportunities," but is not ready to give them everything at once.

Because the fear of unrest in the cities has made many Americans uneasy, this a bad time to pass a powerful civil rights bill. If Congress passes such a law, the public will think that civil rights activists—those who are demanding an immediate change—have intimidated the members of the Senate.

You would defuse resentments and retain the support of most people by looking more toward long-range goals—such as increased opportunity for education and employment—than by enforcing antidiscrimination laws in private businesses. This strategy would reassure white Americans who sympathize with blacks but are concerned about radical changes in society. Even John Kennedy's brother Robert, the U.S. attorney general, has argued at times for restraint. "Some of these people would rather lose the whole bill and lose the legislation" than seek a resolution we all can live with, he complains.

On the other hand, Martin Luther King Jr. points out that because black people have been waiting more than 300 years for their rights, they are understandably impatient. Furthermore, President Johnson has little room to compromise. Because he is a southerner, he believes that people will doubt his commitment to civil rights and will blame him if the bill is weakened in any way. He is determined that this will not happen. And the House of Representatives has pledged not to approve a weakened bill. If you push for a compromise bill, you run a strong risk that no bill will pass.

Finally, in a recent poll more than two-thirds of the voters expressed no confidence in the ability of Congress to do its job. Their main reason for doubt was the Senate's tendency to drag its feet instead of acting quickly and decisively. Another watered-down compromise on this bill will only feed the public's disdain.

YOU ARE A SENATOR.
WHAT IS YOUR DECISION?

Option 1   **Support the civil rights bill.**

Option 2   **Oppose the civil rights bill.**

Option 3   **Work for a compromise bill.**

Senator Hubert Humphrey was elected vice-president with President Lyndon Johnson less than five months after the passage of the Civil Rights Act of 1964.

The Senate chose *Option 1*.

On June 19, 1964, the Senate passed the Civil Rights Act of 1964 by a vote of 73 to 27. President Johnson signed the bill into law on July 2, 1964.

ANALYSIS

One of the immediate effects of the vote was that it hurt the presidential candidacy of Republican senator Barry Goldwater, who was a vocal opponent of the bill. Because most people identified the bill with President Johnson, a

Surrounded by supporters, including senators who were at the forefront of the civil rights debate in Congress, President Lyndon Johnson signs a 1968 civil rights bill.

Democrat, passage of the bill weakened the Democratic Party in the South. In 1968, frustrated southerners bolted from the Democratic Party and rallied behind third-party candidate George Wallace. The erosion of support for the Democratic Party in the South continued in the years that followed.

The bill itself did not end racial discrimination or segregation. But the lawmakers never intended it to be an absolute cure for an extremely difficult and deep-rooted problem. They designed it to outlaw discrimination against blacks and provide means for legal action, and the act accomplished that.

African American leader Roy Wilkins said the main value of the act was the "recognition finally—by the Congress of the United States—that the Negro is a constitutional citizen." While many barriers to economic opportunity for minority citizens have lingered, this recognition has taken root. Today, Americans are far more united in their belief that all people deserve the equal protection of the law as well as equal opportunities in their lives than they were when the bill was passed in 1964.

5

DIRECT ELECTION OF THE PRESIDENT
October 1970

For a nation that champions democracy, the United States has an odd method of electing a president. The winner of the presidential election is not the candidate who collects the most popular votes. Instead, each political party selects a slate of electoral-college delegates, or *electors*, for each state. States get one elector for each of their representatives and senators in Congress. The political party of the candidate who receives the most popular votes in a state sends its group of electors to the electoral college. For example, if the majority of New York voters support the Republican candidate, then only the Republican electors will go to the electoral college to represent New York. While these electors are not legally bound to vote for their party's candidate, they usually do.

The candidate who receives a majority of the votes in the electoral college wins the presidency, regardless of the totals of the national popular vote. If no candidate gets a majority in the electoral college, the House of Representatives chooses the president.

Democratic senator Birch Bayh of Indiana has proposed a constitutional amendment that would change the method of electing the president of the United States. Bayh's plan would eliminate the current electoral college and award the presidency to whichever candidate receives the most popular votes in the election. The proposal also includes a provision to have a special runoff election between the top two vote-getters if no candidate wins at least 40 percent of the popular vote.

BACKGROUND

The electoral-college system has produced some bitter disputes during its history. In 1824, Andrew Jackson defeated several opponents by a wide margin in the popular vote, winning 43 percent of the vote compared to 30.5 percent for his nearest rival, John Quincy Adams. But because more than two strong candidates were running, neither Jackson nor Adams won a majority of the electoral votes. Instead, the election went to the House of Representatives, which elected Adams, even though it seemed clear that the public had preferred Jackson.

In 1876, Democrat Samuel Tilden won 51 percent of the popular vote while Republican Rutherford B.

Hayes received 48 percent. Hayes, however, squeaked out a one-vote victory in the electoral college.

Just 12 years later, President Grover Cleveland, running for reelection on the Democratic ticket, edged Benjamin Harrison in the popular vote, 48.7 percent to 47.9 percent. Yet Harrison, who had received fewer popular votes, won the electoral-college vote by 233 to 168.

Since that time, every winner of the popular vote has also won the electoral-college vote. But concerns over the electoral-college system arose again in 1968. That year, Republican Richard Nixon and Democrat Hubert H. Humphrey ran a tight race for the presidency. At the same time, third-party candidate George Wallace enjoyed strong support in several southern states.

In 1828, four years after John Quincy Adams's controversial election, Andrew Jackson (left) defeated Adams and took office as the nation's seventh president.

Republicans contested the election results in three southern states which the Democratic candidate, Samuel Tilden (left), had won. A special electoral commission decided in Republican Rutherford B. Hayes's favor and he became the president.

In 1892, Grover Cleveland (right) again became president by defeating Republican Benjamin Harrison, who in 1888 had become the president despite losing the popular vote.

Many political experts feared that Wallace would win enough electoral votes to deny both Nixon and Humphrey a majority in the electoral college. If this happened, the election would be turned over to the House of Representatives, where Wallace would be able to offer the votes of his supporters to one of the major-party candidates in exchange for promises to support the programs and policies that he advocated. Although that dreaded outcome did not come to pass—Nixon won a large majority of the electoral votes—many politicians and voters are nervous about continuing to allow the possibility of such electoral disputes. They want to change the system.

Bills to alter the electoral-college system are nothing new. Proposals to reform the system of electing the president have been introduced in almost every session of Congress since the end of the 1700s. Constitutional amendments, however, require a two-thirds majority in Congress to pass, and no such amendment has gained the necessary votes.

In September 1969, the House of Representatives set the latest proposal into motion. By an overwhelming vote of 338 to 70, the House approved a bill proposing a constitutional amendment to scrap the electoral-college system. This bill abolishes states as voting units and relies strictly on the popular vote to determine who is president.

THE DECISION IS YOURS.

How will you vote on the proposed constitutional amendment to eliminate the electoral college and instead elect a president by popular vote?

Option 1 **Support the proposed amendment.**

The electoral-college system is a ridiculous way for a democracy to elect its most important leader. It rests on no noble tradition. The founders of this country grudgingly settled on the electoral-college system only as a compromise between those who wanted direct election by the people and those who wanted Congress to elect the president. Many of the delegates at the Constitutional Convention in 1787 did not trust the public to elect the president. But after almost 200 years of democracy in action, it is clear that this is no longer a concern.

Even in the first few years of presidential elections, the electoral college ran into problems. Congress changed the electoral college after Thomas Jefferson and Aaron Burr each received the same number of electoral votes in the 1800 election, but more crises followed. In 1824, Andrew Jackson's supporters were irate that John Quincy Adams won the election despite the voters' clear choice of Jackson. They accused Adams of buying votes in the House of Representatives to win the election. This suspicion destroyed the public's trust in Adams and made it almost impossible for him to govern effectively.

Rutherford B. Hayes's victory in 1876 also shook the foundations of the government. Samuel Tilden's supporters were outraged that the electoral commission that ruled on the validity of the contested electoral votes had a majority of Republicans on it. They were convinced that Hayes had stolen the election.

Imagine the anger and scorn from the American public that would rain today on a president who lost the popular vote but nonetheless claimed the nation's highest office. The country cannot afford another presidency tainted by such mistrust. Yet under the electoral-college system, the odds of such an event happening are high. In 1968, the United States again narrowly escaped a situation in which American Independent Party candidate George Wallace had enough electoral votes to send the election decision to the House of Representatives.

Besides its basic undemocratic nature, the present system also includes a number of small but important flaws. No matter how tiny its population, each state has at least three electoral votes. This means the least populous states have a higher proportion of electoral votes to voters than do the more populated states.

Many white southerners who had been Democrats supported third-party candidate George Wallace, who believed in segregating blacks and whites, thus helping Republican Richard Nixon win the 1968 presidential election.

For example, in a fair system, if State A has 1.2 million people and State B has 600,000, State A should have twice as many electoral votes as State B. But under the electoral-college system, State A has four electoral votes while State B has three. Therefore, the votes of citizens in State B count for more than the votes of those in State A.

In addition, the winner-take-all system for each state distorts the wishes of the people. It allows for the possibility that a candidate who ekes out razor-thin victories in key states but loses heavily in the other states can win the election despite being trounced in the popular vote. Under the electoral-college system, a candidate could potentially win the presidency while losing the popular vote by a two-to-one margin.

The present system also invites fraud because it allows a few votes to have a huge impact on the election's outcome. For example, if Candidate A beat Candidate B in California by one vote and the president were elected by a national popular vote, there would be no reason for California officials to cheat in counting the vote. After all, one vote in an election of 100 million voters means precious little. Under the present system, however, when the winner in each state gets every electoral vote of that state, a switch of just one vote could transfer all of California's electoral votes from one candidate to the other. Since California has 10 percent of the country's electoral votes, a switch of just one vote could take 10 percent of the vote from one candidate and give it to the other. That is such a significant portion of the total vote that, in most elections, a fraudulent one-vote switch would give the election to the losing candidate.

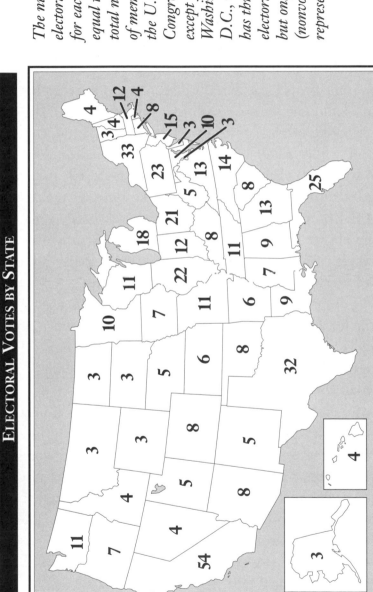

The number of electoral votes for each state is equal to its total number of members in the U.S. Congress, except for Washington, D.C., which has three electoral votes but only one (nonvoting) representative.

Those who worry about the effect of tampering with the long-standing American system of elections can be reassured by looking at the method of electing U.S. senators. For more than a century, state legislators chose their state's senators. In 1913, the country approved a constitutional amendment calling for the direct election of senators by popular vote. That change has worked well.

Some people fear that the direct election of the president would encourage a rash of third-party candidates who would create chaos in American politics. Under the present winner-take-all system, third-party candidates seldom win more than a handful of electoral votes and so have little incentive to run. Even if 20 candidates ran, the top two or three popular vote-getters would usually get all of the electoral votes. This ensures a clear-cut winner. However, if a dozen candidates split the popular vote, the winner might end up with only 20 percent.

The proposed amendment eliminates this fear by calling for a runoff between the top two vote-getters if no candidate gets more than 40 percent of the vote. This will erase the splintering effect of third-party candidates on the total vote.

In short, the proposed amendment would do the fair thing: it would give each citizen an equal vote. This would guarantee that the candidate with the most votes would be the winner. Republican president Richard Nixon endorses this proposal, and many former presidents have supported the idea of direct election. The public also believes this system would be more fair and democratic: voters support this amendment by a landslide margin of more than four to one.

Option 2 **Oppose the proposed amendment.**

Our nation's founders were suspicious of giving too much power to any one group. To ensure that no group gained too much control, they divided the powers and duties of government and varied the methods of election. They intentionally set up different methods of electing different officials. This proposal instead puts all the elective power in the same place—in the popular vote of a public that may or may not be informed.

The proposed amendment would increase, not decrease, the effects of voter fraud. For example, John F. Kennedy won the 1960 election by just 118,550 ballots. Many suspected fraud had aided him in three states. Had the election been decided by popular vote, the entire

After President John F. Kennedy's assassination on November 22, 1963, a survey showed that 65 percent claimed to have voted for him in 1960—a gain of 15 percent over his actual support.

country would have been concerned about the alleged fraud. But thanks to the electoral-college system, corrupt election officials can manipulate the vote only in their own states and thus can have little effect on the total vote. New York and Florida voters, for instance, did not have to wonder if voter fraud in Illinois or Texas had stolen the election. Kennedy had enough electoral votes in states where the results were undisputed to put the issue to rest.

Direct election would also destroy the American tradition of letting each state decide how to govern itself. Some states now have more voting restrictions than others. Under direct election, the voting laws in each state would have to be identical so that states with fewer restrictions would not have an unfair advantage over states with more stringent requirements. Otherwise, those states with fewer restrictions would have many more voters per capita than those with tighter restrictions.

When each state is allotted a certain number of electoral-college votes, local restrictions on voters do not matter. The state of Georgia, for instance, has a certain number of electoral votes even if it makes the voting age 18 and, as a result, has more voters than other states with similar populations that require voters to be at least 21 years old. Direct election would violate the right of states to govern their own affairs.

The electoral-college system gives each state a sense of community identity without violating the principle of democracy. A state sets its own rules for voting and then holds an election to decide which presidential candidate the state prefers. If a majority of the citizens there vote for Candidate A, then that candidate gets all of the state's votes. What could be more fair or democratic? In the words of historian Theodore White, by eliminating this system and going to a popular vote, you would "reduce Americans to faceless digits on an enormous tote board."

Switching to a popular vote would also lower the quality of election campaigns. Currently, candidates must campaign in each region of the country and speak to the particular concerns of each state. Under a popular vote system, candidates would stick to more general issues, and states with large metropolitan areas would get far

Republican senator Roman Hruska of Nebraska calls the direct-election proposal "the most mischievous and dangerous constitutional amendment" ever introduced.

more attention than they do now. Candidates would also pour millions of dollars into national television advertising, which tends to deal in slick packaging rather than substantial ideas.

A racial issue is involved here, too. Under the current system, candidates must appeal to each state's various interest groups in order to win that state's votes. For example, a candidate who ignores the concerns of black voters will have trouble winning in states such as New York and Illinois. Under a direct-vote system, however, candidates do not have to pay much attention to African American concerns. Blacks, after all, make up only about 11 percent of the total national population. Black congressman William Clay, a Democrat from Missouri, fears that a direct vote will destroy any chance that minorities might have of getting candidates to address their needs.

Finally, the runoff election in the event that no candidate gets 40 percent of the vote is a terrible idea because it could increase the cost and length of presidential elections. It would also encourage all sorts of fringe political parties to run candidates in hopes of creating a runoff. Fringe parties could then strike bargains with one of the two front-runners and could gain unfair influence by offering their support in exchange for special favors.

The electoral-college system may be flawed, but it has worked for nearly 200 years. Although power has changed hands many times, the government has remained stable. Predicting all the subtle consequences that may occur if you now try to install a new system of electing the president is impossible. Why tinker with a system that is working so well that it is the envy of much of the world?

Option 3 **Work for a compromise reform.**

Many of the other possible plans to alter the method of electing the president outline changes that could be made to the electoral-college system instead of eliminating it. The two plans that have received the most serious consideration are the district plan and the proportional plan for replacing the current "winner-take-all" method of awarding electoral-college votes.

The district plan treats electors as electoral-college representatives for congressional districts and states. Whichever candidate won the popular vote in a congressional district would be awarded that district's elector, and the candidate who won the statewide popular vote would gain two electors.

The proportional plan simply splits the electoral votes according to the percentage of the popular vote each candidate received. If Candidate A won 20 percent of Minnesota's popular vote, for example, that candidate would gain 2 of Minnesota's 10 electoral votes. Both the district and the proportional plans would be more fair than the current system, in which the winner of the popular vote gets all of the state's electoral votes.

YOU ARE A SENATOR.
WHAT IS YOUR DECISION?

Option 1   **Support the proposed amendment.**

Option 2   **Oppose the proposed amendment.**

Option 3   **Work for a compromise reform.**

Senator Birch Bayh's direct-election proposal languished for months in a Senate committee before Bayh could introduce it to the full Senate.

The Senate killed the bill with a filibuster.

Those opposed to the bill used a technique known as a *filibuster.* Senators debated the issue endlessly until those in favor gave up trying to bring the bill to a vote. Senator Bayh campaigned for several weeks to get the Senate to cut off debate, thus ending the filibuster, and pass his resolution, but he got nowhere. Supporters made their final effort to bring the measure to a vote in early October, but they gave up on October 5, 1970, and conceded defeat. The Senate set aside the proposal and never acted on it. The electoral-college system still remains in place.

ANALYSIS

The direct election of the president is an issue that Americans seldom think about except at election time. Since it does not directly affect their lives, they are not particularly passionate about the issue one way or the other. Therefore, despite continuing public support for direct election, the Senate has never dealt with the issue.

The electoral-college system, meanwhile, continues to create anxious situations for the American public. During the 1992 presidential election, the issue of electoral-college reform surfaced again with the emergence of third-party candidate Ross Perot. Public dissatisfaction with the Republican and Democratic candidates, combined with Perot's wide appeal, created the possibility of another muddied presidential election. Political analysts warned that Perot was capable of getting enough support

When Ross Perot ran for president as a third-party candidate in 1992, he won 19 percent of the popular vote—more than any third-party candidate since Theodore Roosevelt in 1912.

to deny either major-party candidate a majority in the electoral college. If this happened, the election would be thrown into the House of Representatives.

But Perot's support slipped in the later stages of the campaign after he had dropped out and then reentered the contest. He won millions of votes, but he did not win a majority of the popular votes in any state. For this reason, he did not win a single electoral vote, and the Senate was spared yet another round of electoral-college reform bills.

6

WAR POWERS
November 1973

For several years, the United States Congress has been debating various versions of a resolution restricting the president's authority to make war. First introduced in 1971 by Republican senator Jacob Javits of New York and Democratic senator Thomas Eagleton of Missouri, the War Powers resolution that the Senate is now considering would limit the president's power to commit U.S. troops to action without the approval of Congress. The present version of the bill includes the following four major provisions:

    1. The president must consult with Congress in any situation where violence appears likely.

    2. The president must make a formal report to Congress within 48 hours of sending U.S. military forces equipped for combat into a foreign territory or a situation

in which hostilities are likely. This report must say why the action is necessary. It must also include an estimate of how long the operation will last and how much force will be necessary.

3. Congress must then pass a declaration of war within 90 days of the action, or else the action must end.

4. Congress can order a halt to the action at any time by passing a resolution to that effect. The president has no veto power over the resolution.

BACKGROUND

The founders of the United States took great pains to see that the new nation's leaders did not involve the country in war. Because they wanted to ensure that the American people would not be oppressed by an autocratic government, the founders did not even supply the national government with a full-time, standing army for its defense. Such an army would have reminded Americans of the standing armies the British monarchy had kept in the American colonies to control the colonists. Instead, the United States relied on state militias (as in the War of 1812) or on a volunteer army (as in the Mexican War in 1845). With the exception of the Civil War period, the United States kept a very small regular army until well into the twentieth century.

Times have changed, however. In response to threats from Nazi Germany in the 1940s and then from the Soviet Union during the following decade, the United States built up a large permanent military force. That force is so strong and mobile that American leaders can

The United States government ran into serious difficulties during the War of 1812 because many of the governors who controlled the state militias refused to commit their troops to war.

now send warships, bombers, and troops to any destination in the world with just a few hours' notice.

In recent decades, presidents have become bolder about using this force to back U.S. interests in foreign lands. Harry S. Truman committed troops to Korea in 1950, and in 1962 John F. Kennedy imposed a naval blockade on Cuba, both without a declaration of war.

The issue of presidential war powers reached a crisis because of the disastrous U.S. policy in Vietnam. During the 1960s, the United States became involved in a major war in that Southeast Asian country despite the fact that Congress had never declared war. In 1964, Congress had

Because President Harry S. Truman called the Korean War a "police action," he did not need a declaration of war from the United States Congress.

overwhelmingly voted in favor of the Gulf of Tonkin resolution that authorized President Lyndon B. Johnson to "take all necessary measures to repel any armed attacks against the forces of the United States and to prevent further aggression" in Vietnam, but it never again authorized military action in the Vietnam War. The Vietnam War has proven extremely unpopular and has sparked widespread protests throughout the United States.

Gradually, senators grew more outspoken in their opposition to a war that caused such division in the country. They noted that the U.S. Constitution gave Congress the authority to wage war. Yet in Vietnam, first President Johnson and now President Richard Nixon conducted a bloody conflict without a formal declaration of war from Congress. What gave these presidents that right?

The last straw came in May 1970. At that time, President Nixon ordered a heavy bombardment of Cambodia, even though Congress had not declared war against that country. Nixon said the bombing was necessary to defeat the North Vietnamese, who were supplying their forces in South Vietnam through Cambodia. The president took care not to describe the action as an "invasion" of Cambodia because an invasion would require the approval of Congress. Instead, he used the word "incursion," which did not need congressional approval.

At this point, many legislators began to feel that the president had robbed Congress of its constitutional power to declare war. They asked how they had ever let the president involve the American people in such a divisive, unpopular war in the first place. More importantly, they asked how the nation could avoid getting caught up in such a war in the future.

The current proposal is the final product of a three-year legislative effort to find ways of limiting the power of the president to wage undeclared war. Congress wants to limit this power without endangering the security of the United States.

THE DECISION IS YOURS.

How will you vote on the resolution to limit the president's power to conduct military operations?

Option 1 **Support the proposed War Powers resolution.**

This resolution is nothing more than an attempt to enforce the law of the land. The U.S. Constitution clearly states that the president does not have the power to raise armies or to commit them in the field. James Madison, one of the primary architects of the Constitution, left no doubt that this was the intent of the founders when he wrote that the power to declare war, "including the power of judging the causes of war, is fully and exclusively vested in the legislature." The only military authority the Constitution gives to the president is the authority to repel "sudden attacks." James Wilson, one of the other drafters of the Constitution, explained that all war-making powers "are vested in Congress," and the president has only the "authority to lead the army."

Madison discussed the reasoning behind this division of powers. "The Constitution supposes," he explained, "what the history of all Governments demonstrates, that the Executive is the branch of power most interested in war and most prone to it." In order to prevent the president from involving the nation in a war that the people do not want, the founders of the United States gave Congress almost all the powers of declaring and waging war.

For a number of years, U.S. presidents have been skirting this clear division of powers and taking more authority than the Constitution allows. Their main tactic has been to send troops into action for "national security reasons" without any declaration of war. The Vietnam conflict demonstrates how these presidents use "national security" to cover a broad range of circumstances that allow them to send troops to fight wars that are not emergencies. The intense national uproar over the Vietnam War was a result of the president undertaking a military operation in South Vietnam that millions of Americans opposed. This is a prime example of what the writers of the Constitution wanted to avoid.

The War Powers resolution strives to prevent this kind of fiasco from happening again. Under this bill, the president could no longer send American soldiers into a war, such as the Vietnam War, that might last many years and result in tens of thousands of deaths without the explicit backing of the U.S. Congress, the representatives of the American people.

Some critics complain that the resolution is too tough. But they are wrong, for the War Powers resolution gives a president the right to commit troops if a crisis should arise and the country's interests are at stake. The bill simply forces the president to justify this action and to get congressional approval before committing American troops to lengthy and costly wars.

Nor is the bill too lax, as other critics complain. It is not a 90-day blank check giving a president an unlimited right to commit military troops. Congress, after all, retains the right to cut off funds for military action at any time.

What the War Powers resolution provides is a reasonable balance between Congress and the president. It restores Congress's role as the country's authority in deciding whether to wage war, but it does not prevent the president from taking measures to protect the nation.

Because his Vietnam policy was so unpopular, President Lyndon B. Johnson (shown here speaking with U.S. troops in Vietnam) decided not to run for reelection in 1968.

The bill provides a framework for the president and for Congress to work together to decide what kind of military responsibilities the country wants to accept.

Option 2 Oppose this bill and any other war powers resolution.

The Constitution was never meant to be a rule book that contains regulations governing every possible situation that might come up. Alexander Hamilton, one of the most prominent leaders in the early days of the United States, observed, "It is impossible to foresee or define the extent and variety" of crises the nation might face in the future. Since the writers of the Constitution could not predict every possible circumstance that could arise, senators today would be foolish to try to make its words apply to every situation.

Notice that while the Constitution gives Congress the responsibility to declare war, it also gives the president the role of commander-in-chief of the armed forces. In the late twentieth century, the role of the commander-in-chief is vastly different from what it was when the United States was founded.

The modern world is much more dangerous than it used to be. Threats to American security can arise in a flash from thousands of miles away. As a spokesperson for the U.S. State Department says, "An attack on a country far from our shores can impinge directly on the nation's security." In order to protect the security of the United States, the president must have greater power to act decisively against threats.

President Nixon believes that the War Powers resolution is both foolish and unconstitutional. He has told Congress that he is "unalterably opposed to and must veto any bill containing the dangerous and unconstitutional restrictions" on presidential war powers. Sometimes a crisis demands quick action, but Congress, unfortunately, is not designed for quick action. A crisis could get out of control while Congress debates the pros and cons of getting involved.

House Minority Leader Gerald Ford, who has just been nominated to replace Spiro Agnew as President Nixon's vice-president, argues that the U.S. occasionally can prevent outbreaks of war in foreign lands through a quick and decisive show of force. He feels this bill would undermine the president's ability to use such a tactic.

Some political analysts believe this is a particularly bad time to present a bill restraining the chief executive. President Nixon is currently under fire because of suspicions that he was involved in the illegal break-in at the Democratic headquarters in the Watergate building. They maintain that any attempt to remove power from the president now will appear to be a power grab by a Congress that is taking advantage of the president's troubles. President Nixon is appealing to Republican senators to show support for his embattled administration.

Congress's main quarrel with the president does not appear to be with his taking action. Instead, Congress does not like the particular action he took in Cambodia. But just because you as a senator disagree with this president's policy does not give you the right to strip him of the powers of the presidential office. If that were allowed, Congress could threaten to take power from the president any time it disagreed with any presidential policy. Such congressional behavior can only damage the presidency in future years.

Option 3 Work to adopt an even stronger war powers resolution.

The problem with the present resolution is not that it limits the powers of the president too much, but that it grants the president too much power. The U.S. Constitution says the president will *never* raise armies and commit them in the field unless the country is under

Although James Madison (1751-1836) worked to limit the president's authority to engage in military actions, the new nation's first major military conflict, the War of 1812, took place during his presidency and was called "Mr. Madison's War."

attack. Never means never. James Madison declared that only Congress has the right to decide whether or not there is cause to declare war.

The proposed resolution allows the president to sidestep that constitutional order. In effect, the War Powers resolution grants the president permission to take military action without the need for a declaration of war from Congress. It allows the president to commit hundreds of thousands of American soldiers for a limited period of time into situations where they must fight and face a strong possibility of dying.

President Nixon can call this an "incursion" or a "preventative action" or a "peacekeeping mission" or whatever else he wants. The phrase he uses does not change the fact that he is sending American troops to war. This kind of military activity by the president is exactly what the authors of the Constitution worked hard to prevent.

The fact that presidents in recent years have taken such actions without consulting Congress does not justify them. The U.S. Congress should stand up for its constitutional rights. Senator Thomas Eagleton of Missouri, one of the original bill's sponsors, believes the current War Powers resolution is a "Congressional surrender."

Professor Harold Koh of the Yale Law School further notes that the War Powers resolution is vague. Yes, the resolution *sounds* tough in that it requires the president to consult with Congress before entering any situation in which "hostilities are imminent" (any situation that could result in weapons being fired). But, in reality, the bill allows the president to determine whether a certain troop movement is likely to lead to a war.

A president can get around the War Powers resolution by understating the danger involved in a military operation. The resolution also contains loopholes, such as a failure to specify how many legislators the president must consult or exactly what the word "consulting" means. In order to retain as much control as possible and to avoid truly sharing any power with Congress on this issue, a president will interpret the wording of the bill in the narrowest sense.

The current War Powers resolution also says nothing about secret operations conducted by the Central Intelligence Agency (CIA). If the bill does not deal with these types of military actions, the president could undertake secret intelligence operations and claim that the War Powers resolution does not affect them. The president could then justify almost any secret military activities with the vague claim of defending national security.

Finally, critics who say that Congress does not have the wisdom to recognize when the U.S. needs to apply quick military force to protect its interest may be right. But that does not change the issue. The Constitution does not guarantee that Congress will always be smart; nonetheless, it does guarantee Congress the right to make decisions about sending Americans into combat.

YOU ARE A SENATOR.
WHAT IS YOUR DECISION?

Option 1   **Support the proposed War Powers resolution.**

Option 2   **Oppose this bill and any other war powers resolution.**

Option 3   **Work to adopt an even stronger war powers resolution.**

Senator Thomas Eagleton referred to the final version of the War Powers Act he had originally sponsored as "non-binding, non-enforceable."

The Senate chose *Option 1*.

The Senate and the House both passed the War Powers resolution of 1973. On October 24, 1973, President Nixon vetoed the bill on the grounds that it was unconstitutional. That meant that the bill could become law only if two-thirds of those in both houses of Congress voted for the resolution.

On November 7, 1973, Congress did just that. By a vote of 284 to 135, the House of Representatives narrowly approved the resolution. The Senate decisively overrode Nixon's veto by a vote of 75 to 18, and the resolution became law.

ANALYSIS

The War Powers resolution of 1973 succeeded in restoring some military decisions to Congress. In the most dramatic example, President George Bush eventually sought authorization from Congress before opening fire in the 1991 Persian Gulf War against Iraq. This approval gave him solid backing before sending troops into combat.

Some experts argue that the War Powers resolution of 1973 has weakened the country by tying the president's hands in crisis situations. Since then, however, presidents have had little trouble sending troops, ships, and bombers where they wanted to use them. In fact, those who criticized the bill for granting the president too much power proved to be the better forecasters. In 1983, President Ronald Reagan ordered an invasion of the island of Grenada; President Bush invaded Panama in

1989; and President Bill Clinton sent troops to Haiti in 1993—all without declarations of war from Congress.

Furthermore, presidents have used the vague wording and loopholes in the resolution to sidestep its stated purpose. When imposing a military blockade on Iraq prior to the Persian Gulf War, President Bush downplayed the seriousness of the situation. If he had admitted that the situation was so tense that hostilities were inevitable, Congress would have started the clock on the 90 days in which he was permitted to conduct operations without seeking congressional approval. Because he understated the military tensions, Bush was able to set up the blockade without the 90-day countdown even starting.

Presidents also have made frequent use of their national security spy operations to get around the War Powers resolution. When he was the CIA director, William Colby justified a number of military actions by noting that the War Powers resolution did not apply to secret intelligence operations. CIA employees, claimed Colby, were not a part of the military.

More than 20 years after the War Powers resolution took effect, critics continue to hammer away at it. Some call it a "congressional cave-in." According to one political analyst, "Far from putting a congressional clamp on Presidential wars, the resolution actually encourages such ventures by allowing the President to dispatch American troops for up to 90 days without the slightest nod from Congress."

7

BALANCING THE BUDGET
September 1985

The federal government frequently spends more money than it collects from taxes and other sources. When the government engages in this *deficit spending*, it borrows the difference and pays interest on the debt. Sometimes such spending is justified to fund wars or to get the nation through a financial crisis. Other times, Congress is simply funding pet projects or avoiding politically difficult cuts due to pressure from constituents or special-interest groups. In recent years, the government debt has been spiraling out of control, and many people believe it is time to rein it in.

The Senate is considering a proposal by Republican senators Phil Gramm of Texas and Warren Rudman of New Hampshire and Democratic senator Ernest Hollings of South Carolina that would force Congress to spend no more money each year than the Treasury collects in taxes. The Gramm-Rudman-Hollings bill sets a five-year target for reaching the goal of a balanced budget. As Senator Gramm explains, "It requires the president to submit and Congress to pass budgets that reduce the federal deficit by $36 billion annually for the next five years."

If Congress has failed to meet the goal of a $36-billion reduction on October 1 in each of the next five years, the president must make spending cuts in a wide range of programs in order to reach that goal. These cuts must affect each program equally so that no area of the government has to bear an unfair burden of budget cuts.

BACKGROUND

Deficit spending can serve a good purpose. Individuals, for example, seldom have enough money to purchase their first house outright. Instead, they borrow the money and pay it back with interest over the years. If they do this, they can enjoy a house now rather than wait many years until they have saved the entire purchase price. Governments also borrow money to finance major projects. In addition, they spend a great deal of money to buy goods and services during times when business is slow, which helps to boost the economy.

Unfortunately, deficit spending has gotten out of hand in the past decade. In 1970, the federal government spent about $3 billion more than it collected. But times have changed, and so has the deficit. The budget deficit for 1986 will probably be over $200 billion. And the rate of increase shows no signs of slowing down.

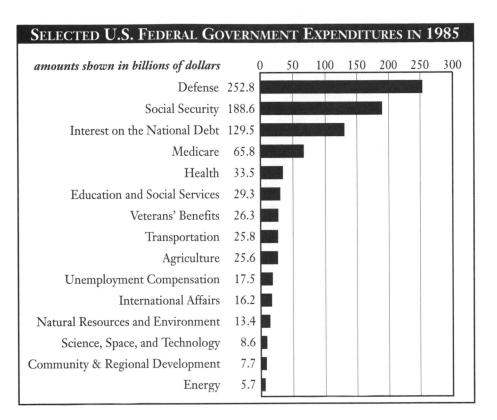

SELECTED U.S. FEDERAL GOVERNMENT EXPENDITURES IN 1985

amounts shown in billions of dollars

Defense	252.8
Social Security	188.6
Interest on the National Debt	129.5
Medicare	65.8
Health	33.5
Education and Social Services	29.3
Veterans' Benefits	26.3
Transportation	25.8
Agriculture	25.6
Unemployment Compensation	17.5
International Affairs	16.2
Natural Resources and Environment	13.4
Science, Space, and Technology	8.6
Community & Regional Development	7.7
Energy	5.7

The total amount spent by the U.S. government in 1985 was almost $1 trillion. About half went to defense, Social Security, and interest payments on the growing national debt. There would be a financial crisis if the U.S. defaulted on its loan payments.

Total debt in the United States has now reached nearly $2 trillion, which is roughly $8,000 for every man, woman, and child in the country. Interest on that debt is mounting every day.

U.S. citizens have two major concerns with the huge debt that the federal government is amassing. First, such a rate of deficit spending is unfair to our children and grandchildren. This growing debt allows our current generation to enjoy many benefits without paying for them, but future generations will have to pay off our debt. The public in the future will not only have to pay its own bills; it will have to pay ours as well.

Second, the mushrooming deficit is crowding out all other spending. One of the largest items in the current budget is interest payments on the debt. As we pile up more debt, the interest payments climb. We are fast approaching the point where Congress will either have to raise taxes dramatically to provide the money for these interest payments or make drastic cuts in government spending. If nothing is done, the nation will eventually spend all its tax money for the interest on the national debt and will not be able to provide for defense, Social Security, or any other programs.

The difficult part about cutting federal spending to a manageable figure is that you cannot cut without getting rid of programs that a large number of American citizens support. Any time you eliminate a program or a benefit that a voter is accustomed to receiving, you run the risk of infuriating that voter. Most senators are convinced they cannot win reelection if they anger a large segment of voters. Since no one likes to lose elections, senators are often reluctant to cut programs. And so the deficit continues to grow.

Few Americans doubt the seriousness of this situation. Even Massachusetts senator Edward Kennedy, who strongly supports government spending for a wide variety of programs, calls for deficit reduction. The only way to guarantee that important government programs continue to have funds to operate is to get the debt under control.

Democratic senator Edward Kennedy fought unsuccessfully to save Medicare and Medicaid from the 1986 budget cuts. These programs provide health-care funding for elderly and low-income citizens.

The Gramm-Rudman bill is an attempt to solve this dilemma by forcing Congress to reduce the deficit. Its key feature is across-the-board spending cuts in a wide range of programs so that no special-interest groups can complain about being singled out for sacrifice.

THE DECISION IS YOURS.

How will you vote on the Gramm-Rudman plan to force Congress to meet deficit-reduction goals?

Option 1 Oppose the Gramm-Rudman bill.

Bills such as Gramm-Rudman are worthless gimmicks that allow Congress to avoid taking responsibility.

The way for Congress to balance the budget is to stop talking and actually balance it! That will take courage and honesty, not budget gimmickry.

Congress can easily get around the Gramm-Rudman provisions the same way it has skirted such provisions in the past. In 1978 and 1980, the Senate passed bills stating that, beginning in 1981, the total expenses of the government could no longer exceed its revenue. If you can make Congress balance the budget with legislation, these laws should have solved the problem.

But when budget-cutting got too difficult, Congress simply passed a budget with a larger deficit. This was possible because in Congress the most recent law overrules previous laws. By passing a budget with a deficit, Congress simply overruled the old law. The members of Congress will likely do that again with Gramm-Rudman.

Legal scholars argue that Gramm-Rudman violates the Constitution because it forces the executive branch of the U.S. government to make designated budget cuts if Congress fails to meet its targets. The Constitution clearly gave the power to set the budget to Congress, not to the president.

Many senators who consider the budget deficit a critical problem believe that Gramm-Rudman makes too many compromises to be effective. Supposedly, the bill calls for widespread mandatory budget cuts. But actually the cuts will affect only a portion of the budget. The bill does not touch interest on the national debt, Social Security, or vital programs such as Medicaid and veterans' benefits. Combined, these expenses account for nearly half of all federal spending.

Everyone can see that Congress cannot reduce a $200-billion yearly deficit without cutting Social Security and other popular programs. If the Gramm-Rudman proposal does not cut Social Security and these other programs, it cannot achieve a balanced budget, and the bill will hamper the work of the federal government without achieving its stated goal.

Democratic senator Gary Hart of Colorado argues that the Gramm-Rudman ax would fall most heavily on certain areas of the budget, such as education, transportation, and health. Although cosponsor Senator Hollings is a Democrat and many Democrats support the bill, this concern has led some Democrats to oppose Gramm-Rudman. Supporters of the bill say that you can address this problem by passing a balanced budget. But if passing a balanced budget were so simple, you would not need Gramm-Rudman in the first place!

Republican representative Dick Cheney of Wyoming warns that while voting for drastic deficit-reduction measures will be popular in the short run, it may cause problems down the road. The members of Congress have not dealt effectively with deficit reduction because they fear public reaction to the resulting tax increases or spending cuts in defense or popular social programs. "If Gramm-Rudman passes, we'll all go through the wringer next year," predicts Cheney.

The rigid provisions of Gramm-Rudman could lead to an economic recession or even a widespread depression that would paralyze the country. When the economy slows down, businesses and individuals make less money and, as a result, pay less in taxes on their earnings. This means a drop in the government's income. At the same time, unemployment usually rises. Because most unemployed people receive some money from the government to live on, government expenses go up.

Therefore, during poor economic times, the government's income goes down while its expenses go up. Gramm-Rudman would force the government either to cut spending even further or else raise taxes to keep the budget balanced.

Financial experts agree that either move would hurt the country. When business is slow, government spending can take up the slack. But if the government cuts spending at such times, business will go into an even greater slump, and there will be no emergency money for those who are laid off work. If the government raises taxes in tough times, it puts an even greater financial burden on businesses and individuals who are already struggling to survive. In such a situation, the only solution is to run a deficit until the economy improves.

Option 2 **Support the Gramm-Rudman bill.**

Most Americans favor deficit reduction and a balanced budget. Senator Rudman calls his bill "a bad idea whose time has come." What he means is that the government should not have to pass such a bill. Congress and the American people would be better off making individual decisions about how much money each program should receive. Instead, this law will automatically cut all programs if Congress does not meet the deficit-reduction goals. A law should not have to limit the options of the American public.

But Rudman recognizes that Congress is incapable of balancing the budget under the current budget rules. Its members lack the will to do what has to be done. Nor has the president shown any inclination to treat seriously the problem of deficit reduction. President Ronald Reagan, a Republican, will not cut defense spending, and Democrats insist that Social Security remain untouched. These items account for nearly half of all government spending. At the same time, Reagan refuses to agree to any tax hikes. There is no way that you will ever achieve a balanced budget under these conditions.

Senator Rudman now sees "a certain sense of despair around here that the major problems facing the country have not been faced." Like many other Republicans, Representative E. Clay Shaw of Florida agrees, saying that "now is the time to act, even if it's in desperation." If

Representative E. Clay Shaw would later become a leading proponent of welfare reform in an effort to reduce government spending.

Congress and the American people refuse to come to grips with reality, then a tough law is needed to force them to do so for the good of the country. Republican senator Robert Packwood of Oregon also believes that the Gramm-Rudman bill will be good for the country because it will force Americans to make decisions about priorities. In the long run, this will give citizens a better idea of what they want and can expect from their government.

Although critics of the Gramm-Rudman bill say it strips Congress of its constitutional power to make budget decisions, the bill does no such thing. As Senator Gramm puts it, "What it does is reduce the power of the President and Congress to *fail* to make decisions." Congress remains free to deal with the problem of deficit spending any way it chooses as long as it does deal with it.

In fact, the proposed bill may give Congress more freedom by removing the harsh realities of politics from the budget process. The bill targets all budget items equally, including both defense programs favored by some and social programs favored by others. Senators will be able to slash spending without getting into stubborn fights about which parts of the budget are most important.

Critics of the Gramm-Rudman proposal maintain that the bill will hit poor people the hardest. By forcing spending cuts in all areas of government, this legislation will undercut programs that the poor, the sick, and the unemployed desperately need to survive. But, again, Gramm-Rudman does not force Congress to make cuts in these areas. If Congress is serious about funding certain programs, it can keep them intact. All it has to do is pass a budget that meets the deficit-reduction targets.

Gramm-Rudman, in fact, may be a painless way of getting rid of costly programs that only powerful special-interest groups support. If the law forces Congress to make the necessary across-the-board cuts, special-interest groups cannot attack any senator or group of senators for opposing them. The senators will simply be following the law.

Finally, Gramm-Rudman will boost the economy. Economic experts have been worried about the effect of huge deficits on the purchasing power of the American consumer. Banking experts say that if Congress shows it is serious about deficit reduction and passes Gramm-Rudman, then fears over the economy will ease. Interest rates will go down, production will increase, and sales will rise.

Option 3 Support an even tougher balanced-budget measure—a constitutional amendment.

Clearly, Congress lacks the will to balance the budget by itself. Even if you pass Gramm-Rudman, Congress can reverse itself and sneak out of the law's requirements. As Speaker of the House Thomas P. "Tip" O'Neill says, whatever Congress enacts last is the law. What is to stop Congress from overriding Gramm-Rudman with a weaker law once the going gets tough?

Congress needs a balanced-budget measure with some teeth. A large majority of Americans support the idea of a balanced-budget amendment. A constitutional amendment requiring Congress to pass a balanced budget each year would provide the discipline that Congress needs to restrain its own spending. Amendments are

Massachusetts Democrat "Tip" O' Neill charged that President Reagan's 1986 budget "takes the pain of budget-cutting directly to middle America."

difficult to pass because they require a two-thirds majority in both the House of Representatives and the Senate as well as approval by three-fourths of the state legislatures. But once such an amendment is in place, Congress cannot repeal it without passing another amendment. This would require overwhelming support from the public.

A requirement that the government balance its budget each year is nothing new. At the present time, 43 states operate under such a restriction and still provide necessary services to their citizens.

Those opposed to a constitutional amendment say it will encourage the government to use accounting tricks and numbers-juggling to claim it is balancing the budget. The amendment will simply be window dressing to make voters feel as though Congress is doing something about the budget. These critics say the American people should not toy with the U.S. Constitution every time they have a problem with government.

Detractors also say this amendment would upset the delicate balance of the government branches that was established by the founders of this country. The legislature is supposed to determine the budget. Under this amendment, if Congress fails to come up with a balanced budget, the courts would step in to enforce the law. Judges who are not directly accountable to the people would then make decisions about how the federal government spends its money.

YOU ARE A SENATOR.
WHAT IS YOUR DECISION?

Option 1   **Oppose the Gramm-Rudman bill.**

Option 2   **Support the Gramm-Rudman bill.**

Option 3   **Support an even tougher balanced-budget measure—a constitutional amendment.**

Republican senators Phil Gramm (left) and Warren Rudman (center) worked closely with Democrat Ernest Hollings (right) to show voters that balancing the federal budget concerned leaders of both parties.

President Ronald Reagan signs the Gramm-Rudman Act. Although President Reagan consistently called for reductions in government spending, deficits increased dramatically during his administration.

The Senate chose *Option 2*.

The Senate passed the Gramm-Rudman bill on September 29, 1985. On December 12, 1985, they also passed a revised version of the bill that better conformed to federal court requirements. President Ronald Reagan signed both measures into law.

ANALYSIS

The Gramm-Rudman Act appeared to have an immediate effect. While federal spending had risen 10 percent each year from 1980 to 1985, it rose only 3.4 percent in the year following the passage of the law. When Congress passed the bill, the year's budget deficit was over $221 billion, or more than 5 percent of the total economic output of the United States. By 1987, the deficit had shrunk to 3.6 percent of the economic output.

But much of that initial improvement turned out to be only an illusion. One analyst stated that both Congress and the president's staff resorted to a range of accounting practices in order to mask the true deficit. Democratic representative Lee Hamilton of Indiana noted that Congress had "developed considerable skill and sophistication in meeting deficit-reducing targets—without reducing the deficit."

In the long run, Gramm-Rudman did not reduce the national debt. Deficit spending actually swelled to around $200 billion each year in the years following the bill's passage. By the end of 1996, the total national debt was projected to exceed $5 trillion—more than double what it was when the Senate enacted Gramm-Rudman. This total is roughly $20,000 for every American.

Despite economists' doubts about the wisdom of amending the Constitution for budgetary reasons, some groups still demand that Congress pass a constitutional amendment. Such an amendment failed to pass the Senate by one vote in 1986 and by two votes in 1995.

A clear majority of Americans continue to support the passage of a balanced-budget amendment. Most Americans, however, *oppose* a balanced-budget amendment if it would require cuts in Social Security. This mixed message has produced a logjam in Congress, where politicians from both parties tend to oppose any cuts that might anger their constituents or financial backers.

8

GUN CONTROL
November 1993

Many Americans view violent crime as one of the most serious problems in the United States today. Handguns play a major role in much of this violent crime. On average, one American is shot every 14 minutes. Each year, criminals use handguns to commit well over half a million crimes.

The statistics are especially devastating when compared to those of other highly industrialized nations. In 1990, the United States reported 10,567 handgun murders. In that same year, the United Kingdom suffered only 22 and Australia only 10.

For nearly seven years, senators have argued the merits of the so-called Brady bill. This proposed law would require those purchasing a handgun to wait five days before taking possession of the gun. During this waiting period, law-enforcement officials would conduct a background check to see whether the buyer had a criminal record that would disqualify him or her from owning a handgun. The waiting period would also prevent dangerous or emotionally distraught people from having immediate access to a lethal weapon.

BACKGROUND

This bill is named for James Brady, who had been President Ronald Reagan's press secretary. When John Hinckley tried to assassinate President Reagan in 1981, Brady was hit by gunfire and suffered a severe head injury and permanent brain damage. Since surviving that crime, Brady and his wife, Sarah, have been in the forefront of gun-control efforts.

Press Secretary James Brady with President Ronald Reagan one month before both were wounded.

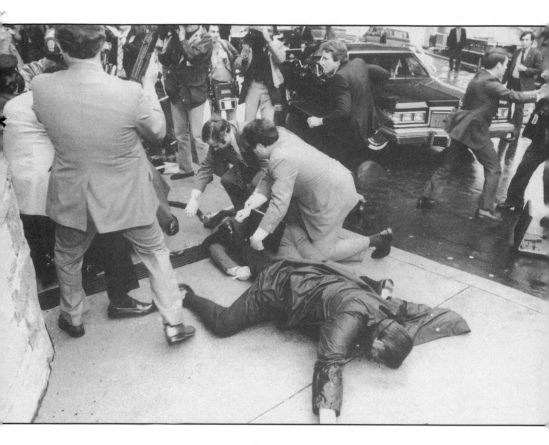

Seconds after the March 30, 1981, attempt on President Reagan's life by gunman John Hinckley, Secret Service agents rush Reagan to the hospital. Officer Thomas Delahanty lies wounded while two agents kneeling behind him help James Brady.

The shameful statistics on handgun violence have prompted many Americans to demand legislation that will attack the problem of violent crime. Proposed solutions include harsher penalties for criminals, more law enforcement officers, and social programs to combat the causes of crime. The proposals that produce the most intense debate are those calling for restrictions on the availability of guns.

Such proposals always run into fierce opposition from the National Rifle Association (NRA) and other organizations. Members of this group believe that the government should not place any restrictions on gun ownership. They defend their position by citing the Second Amendment to the United States Constitution. This amendment states: "A well regulated Militia, being necessary to the security of a free State, the right of the people to keep and bear Arms shall not be infringed." When the Second Amendment was drafted, there was no national army, and the American people needed to be armed to provide for their own defense.

The American Bar Association and many legal scholars, including former Supreme Court chief justice Warren Burger, argue that the Second Amendment is a collective right of the American public, not an individual right. Much of the battle over gun control has centered on the meaning of the constitutional right to bear arms.

Because of such powerful organized opposition, few gun-control proposals ever reach the floor of the Senate. In fact, the U.S. Congress has not passed any significant gun-control measures since 1968, when it enacted a ban on the sale of rifles through the mail.

The Brady bill is the latest battleground between the forces that favor and those that oppose gun control. Since the bill was first introduced in Congress on February 4, 1987, the fight over the proposed legislation has dragged on for more than six years. The House of Representatives passed the Brady bill by the relatively narrow margin of 238 to 189 on November 19, 1993. Now the bill has come before the Senate.

THE DECISION IS YOURS.

How will you vote on the Brady bill, which would require a five-day waiting period and a criminal background check before gun buyers can take possession of their weapons?

Option 1 **Oppose the Brady bill as a violation of individual rights.**

The Second Amendment to the U.S. Constitution guarantees all citizens the right to own weapons. The waiting period that this bill calls for may seem like only a minor nuisance, but, in fact, it violates the right of citizens to bear arms. The problem is not so much the inconvenience of the five-day wait as the example that this kind of provision would set. Once you make one exception to a guaranteed legal right, you open up the possibility for more and more restrictions.

There are active, vocal segments of society and powerful special-interest groups, such as the NRA, that oppose any form of gun control because they believe these restrictions threaten their constitutional rights. Most Republican legislators agree with them. These people consider this issue so important that they not only funnel large campaign contributions to the opponents of gun control, but many also show increasing support for private militias (loosely organized groups of people who train as if they were soldiers). These feelings run especially high in rural western and southern states.

If you are not careful, gun-control advocates will keep chipping away at gun owners' rights little by little. Each time they claim that they are imposing only a petty restriction that has little effect on law-abiding citizens. Gradually, however, advocates of gun control could erode our legal rights. And then, when it is too late to do anything, our rights will be gone.

The federal government has no business telling state and local officials how to run their affairs. If the majority of citizens in a community want to require background checks and waiting periods for handgun purchases, they can urge their state government to pass laws and ordinances to that effect. Background checks are also costly, and they surely invade the privacy of decent citizens. The federal government should not require communities to spend their time and resources to undertake these background checks if local government officials do not believe they are necessary.

Even though Republican senator Bob Smith of New Hampshire had witnessed some brutal murders outside the CIA headquarters in January 1993, he opposed the Brady bill, saying that the gunman, not the weapon, had committed the crime.

Advocates of gun control are making scapegoats out of law-abiding handgun owners by blaming them for the problem of violent crime in America. Based on his research, Gary Kleck, a professor of criminology at Florida State University, argues that most gun-control restrictions have absolutely no effect on the level of violence in a community. NRA vice-president Wayne LaPierre says, "The whole debate over gun control is a public fraud in terms of doing anything in the world that affects violent criminals."

The Brady bill will not accomplish anything meaningful. Most criminals do not buy weapons at licensed gun stores. According to one survey, criminals illegally obtain more than 90 percent of the weapons they use to commit violent crimes. Therefore, the waiting period and background check will only affect responsible citizens.

In fact, the bill would probably increase violent crime by limiting the ability of citizens to buy firearms to defend themselves. The high murder rates in the United States show that the police are not able to protect citizens from violent crime. In an increasingly violent society, the government must allow individuals to defend themselves, and personal firearms are one of the most effective means of protecting citizens from violent crime. Kleck's research shows that Americans successfully defend themselves with firearms about a million times each year.

A study from the Bureau of Justice Statistics indicates that only one in five crime victims who use a gun for defense suffers serious injury. But almost half of those who try to defend themselves without a gun are injured. Criminals often say they are less likely to mug someone or burglarize a home if they believe the intended victim has a gun.

The five-day waiting period that the Brady bill requires could put law-abiding citizens at risk. Suppose an urban area erupts in riots and looting? People who suddenly need a gun to defend their homes or businesses from attack would have to wait five days before getting the weapons they need to protect themselves.

Remember that guns don't kill people, people do. A far better approach to curbing violent crime would be to crack down on criminals by handing down stiffer prison terms for using a weapon in committing a crime and to increase funding for law enforcement.

Option 2 Support the Brady bill.

Despite the fact that the majority of Americans respect the constitutional amendment that guarantees the right to bear arms, more than 70 percent of those surveyed in a recent *Time* magazine poll, especially people living in urban areas with high murder rates, favored some form of legislation regulating handguns.

As sociologist Stephen Klineberg of Rice University in Houston, Texas, explains, "Most Americans are against taking away the rights of individuals to own a gun. But what they're increasingly demanding is rational control over guns." Apparently, the mood of the country favors a moderate form of legislation such as the Brady bill. Most Democrats believe the Brady bill should be passed as a reasonable restriction on handguns.

The dire warnings of the gun advocates notwithstanding, this is not a radical bill that infringes on the

Representative F. James Sensenbrenner Jr. of Wisconsin, a major backer of the Brady bill, was one of only four House Republicans to vote for its passage.

rights of law-abiding citizens while leaving criminals to run free. It is a modest step, designed to keep guns out of the hands of dangerous people while respecting citizens' right to own firearms. In the mid-1970s, even the National Rifle Association had endorsed a waiting period.

In fact, many states already require background checks and waiting periods for those who purchase handguns. Studies in 25 states requiring a waiting period and background check reveal that from one to two percent of prospective purchasers are turned away. While this percentage may seem insignificant, the numbers indicate that the checks protect a potentially large number of people from violent crime. In California alone, each year more than 5,000 criminals who attempt to purchase a gun in violation of the law have been prevented from doing so.

According to Commander David Gascon of the Los Angeles Police Department, "Those guns are being kept out of the hands of people who have the potential to really cause tremendous problems in our society."

While some claim that gun control is an issue that is best left to the individual states, we have to remember that guns do not recognize borders. New York might require a waiting period and a background check for the purchase of a handgun. But what good does a gun-control law in that state do if the customer can buy a firearm in a neighboring state with no questions asked?

Arthur Kellermann, director of the Center for Injury Control at Emory University in Atlanta, Georgia, disputes claims that handguns provide individuals with an important measure of protection. His studies show that guns in the home are 43 times more likely to result in the death of a family member or friend than a criminal. Another study has found that homicides occur 3 times more often in homes in which guns are present. The U.S. Census Bureau further notes that guns are 14 times more likely to be used in committing a crime than for self-defense.

Even Gary Kleck, who argues that guns are a deterrent to crime, has come out in favor of background checks. According to Kleck, such screening "appears to reduce homicide and suicide." Many murders and suicides occur when people are in agitated states. Waiting periods prevent people from purchasing handguns in a murderous or suicidal state of mind. By the time the waiting period has passed, the person is often calmer and less likely to commit a dangerous act.

Granted, the Brady bill will not have a major effect on crime. But the growing level of violence in our society demands some kind of action. In recent years, gunshot wounds have become the leading cause of death for teenage boys. Senators cannot just sit by and allow this to happen without making some kind of action, even if the action is only symbolic. You must do something.

Conservative political analyst William F. Buckley points out that even if the Brady bill doesn't accomplish much, it signals that the government recognizes that violence is a serious problem. Given the clout of the fierce opponents of gun control in our society, this is probably as strong a gun-control measure as Congress will pass.

Option 3 Hold out for tougher gun-control legislation.

Because he believes we must do all we can to reduce the availability of guns, Rhode Island senator John Chafee has twice introduced a bill that would outlaw the manufacture, sale, and possession of handguns. Contrary to the claims of gun-control opponents, similar legislation has been effective. The United Kingdom, Australia, and Japan—three countries that suffer only a small fraction of the murders that the U.S. endures—have tight restrictions on the sale and possession of handguns.

For those who claim that other differences account for the lower violent crime rate, Kellermann points to a study comparing Vancouver, British Columbia, and Seattle, Washington—two cities in the Pacific Northwest. Vancouver has far more restrictions on handguns than does Seattle. Despite similar overall crime rates, the murder rate in

Republican senator John Chafee of Rhode Island goes much farther than most Americans would on handgun restriction, proposing an outright ban on such weapons.

Seattle is much greater than that of Vancouver. Ever since Canada instituted tighter controls on guns in 1978, the risk of dying there from gunfire has dropped.

The argument that guns do not kill people is simplistic. There are about 67 million handguns lying around the United States. All these easily available weapons give people who otherwise might not be dangerous the firepower to kill and maim in the heat of passion.

The argument that we can reduce violent crime by "getting tough" on criminals is equally simplistic. Kleck observes that "a long series of get-tough strategies have been tried, carefully evaluated, and found to be either ineffective . . . or hopelessly expensive."

Organizations concerned with children and health, such as the American Academy of Pediatrics, endorse Chafee's bill. For a major problem like gun control, why settle for an ineffective Band-Aid like the Brady bill when far more effective solutions are available? For the sake of the children who live in fear in many inner-city neighborhoods, the Senate must take stronger action.

YOU ARE A SENATOR.
WHAT IS YOUR DECISION?

Option 1 **Oppose the Brady bill as a violation of individual rights.**

Option 2 **Support the Brady bill.**

Option 3 **Hold out for tougher gun-control legislation.**

*Democratic senator Herb Kohl of Wisconsin, a chief
sponsor of the Brady bill, has also drafted a law that
bans handgun possession by people under age 18.*

Although President George Bush worked with the NRA to block the Brady bill in 1991, he cancelled his membership in the association after the NRA, in an April 1995 fundraising letter, referred to Alcohol, Tobacco, and Firearms agents as "jack-booted thugs" who "murder law-abiding citizens."

The Senate chose *Option 2*.

The Republicans led a *filibuster*—an extended debate to prevent a bill from coming to a vote—on the Brady bill. On November 19, 1993, the Senate voted twice on motions to end the filibuster and bring the bill to a vote. Although a majority of senators voted to end debate, the motion failed both times to win the two-thirds majority required to end the debate. At that point, political analysts believed the bill had no chance of passing.

Strong public reaction against the filibuster, however, led some Republican senators to change their minds overnight. On November 20, 1993, the Senate approved the Brady bill by a vote of 63 to 36. Forty-seven Democrats and 16 Republicans voted in favor, and 8 Democrats and 28 Republicans voted against the bill.

Legislative leaders ironed out minor differences between the House and Senate versions of the bill. Both legislative bodies approved the final version on November 24, 1993.

ANALYSIS

The Brady bill sparked some legal battles, with local authorities claiming the federal government had no power to require a background check. Courts in Montana backed the local authorities while courts in Texas upheld the law. No court in any state ruled against the legality of the waiting period.

The immediate effect of the Brady bill was the opposite of what the lawmakers had intended: it increased the sales of handguns. Many who either misunderstood the law or had concerns about the waiting period or the background check bought handguns just before the law went into effect. Passage of the bill increased the fears of avid gun owners because they thought the government meant to disarm them in violation of the Constitution. Such fears probably also strengthened the formation of private, heavily armed militias of people who are highly suspicious of the government.

As almost everyone had predicted, the bill did not have a dramatic effect on crime. Federal agents reported that the background checks stopped nearly five percent of handgun purchases in the first months after the Brady

James Brady gives the "thumbs-up" to celebrate President Bill Clinton's signing the Brady bill into law on November 30, 1993.

bill was passed. But soon that figure declined to the levels that most states with waiting periods and background checks had previously experienced.

Even so, the Brady bill accomplished Congress's modest goals. The bill certainly did not make dangerous streets safe. But with thousands of gun sales prevented, the new law no doubt did save some lives and stop some crimes.

The passage of the Brady bill has not stopped the debate over gun control, and opponents of gun control continue to work to repeal restrictions on gun ownership. Whenever gun-control issues arise, the National Rifle Association and militia groups proclaim that the U.S. government is trampling on the constitutional rights of its citizens.

HOW A BILL BECOMES A LAW

A U.S. senator or representative introduces a bill, which is assigned to the Senate or the House committee responsible for legislation on that subject. The Senate Judiciary Committee, the House Armed Services Committee, and the Senate Finance Committee are some of the committees.

Committee members debate the bill and may make changes to it. They then vote on the bill.

If the committee approves the bill, it is introduced in the Senate or the House. The senators or representatives debate the bill, often *amending*, or changing, it. Then they vote on it.

If the bill passes, it will go through the same process in the other house of Congress.

If both the Senate and the House approve the bill, members of each house meet to discuss any differences in their versions of the bill. Once they reach an agreement, the bill is sent to the president.

The president has three options: sign the bill into law, veto it, or not sign it. An unsigned bill becomes a law in 10 days unless fewer than 10 days remain in that session of Congress. (This is called a "pocket veto" because it is as if the bill were tucked away in the president's pocket.) The president may also veto sections of a bill but still sign the bill into law. This action is called a line-item veto.

There are many ways for you to learn about and participate in the political process.

• Write (or e-mail) your congressional representatives
about issues that are important to you:

Senator _____   Representative _____
United States Senate   U.S. House of Representatives
Washington, DC 20510   Washington, DC 20515

Internet sites:

U.S. Senate Information:
HTTP://policy.net/capweb/Senate/Senate.html

U.S. House of Representatives Information:
HTTP://policy.net/capweb/House/House.html

• You can look up the voting records and speeches of senators and representatives in *The Congressional Record.*
Congressional Quarterly Almanac summarizes the background, debates, and actions on all major legislation.
These are available at many libraries. You can also read
about what is going on in Congress on the Internet.

• Volunteer for the local branch of the national political
party and of other national organizations that you support. You can also join or form a club at your school.

• Read the newspaper and magazines to keep informed
about current events. Write letters to the editor about
issues that concern you. And encourage your parents to
get involved in politics—especially by voting!

SOURCE NOTES

Quoted passages are noted by page and order of citation.

pp. 18, 24, 29: John Kobler, *Ardent Spirits: The Rise and Fall of Prohibition* (New York: Putnam, 1973).

p. 19 (both): Roger A. Bruns, *Preacher: Billy Sunday and Big-Time American Evangelism* (New York: Norton, 1992).

p. 37: Raymond Moley, *The First New Deal* (New York: Harcourt, Brace & World, 1966).

p. 44: Charles McKinley and Robert W. Frase, *Launching Social Security: A Capture-and-Record Account, 1935-1937* (Madison: University of Wisconsin Press, 1970).

pp. 54 (1st and 2nd), 57: James T. Patterson, *Mr. Republican: A Biography of Robert A. Taft* (Boston: Houghton Mifflin, 1972).

p. 54 (3rd): John Steele Gordon, "Farewell to Taft-Hartley: The Great, Heroic American Labor Movement—How It Became Obsolete," *American Heritage*, October 1994.

p. 55: Margaret Truman, *Harry S. Truman* (New York: William Morrow, 1973).

pp. 70 (1st), 71, 74 (both), 77, 80: Charles W. Whalen and Barbara Whalen, *The Longest Debate: A Legislative History of the 1964 Civil Rights Act* (Cabin John, Md.: Seven Locks Press, 1985).

p. 70 (2nd): Lyndon Johnson, *Public Papers of the Presidents: Lyndon Johnson, 1963-1964* (Washington, D.C.: U.S. Government Printing Office, 1965).

p. 73: "The Debate on Civil Rights: Senator Humphrey vs. Senator Thurmond," *U.S. News & World Report*, March 30, 1964.

p. 75: David Lawrence, "The Big Change," *U.S. News & World Report*, March 30, 1964.

p. 76: "Mood of America in Election Year," *U.S. News & World Report*, March 30, 1964.

p. 93 (1st): Theodore H. White, "Direct Elections: An Invitation to National Chaos," *Life*, January 30, 1970.

p. 93 (2nd): *Congressional Quarterly Almanac: 91st Congress, 2nd Session, 1970*, vol. XXVI (Washington, D.C.: Congressional Quarterly, 1971).

p. 102: James A. Henretta, et al., *America's History*, 2nd ed. (New York: Worth Publishers, 1993).

pp. 104 (1st), 110: Robert K. Musil, "Congressional Giveaway: Troops for a Five-Star President," *Nation*, February 28, 1976.

pp. 104 (2nd and 3rd), 106-107, 107 (1st): Raoul Berger, "On Wars and Treaties: The Constitution Is Clear Enough," *Nation*, March 26, 1973.

pp.107 (2nd), 112: John Lehman, *Making War* (New York: Charles Scribner's Sons, 1992).

p. 114: James A. Goodman, "Presidential Battalions: The Power of the 'Undeclared War,'" *Nation*, February 14, 1976.

p. 121: Jeffrey L. Shelar et al., "Nothing but Tough Choices," *U.S. News & World Report*, November 25, 1985.

p. 122: Paul Magnusson, "Gramm-Rudman Isn't a 'Fiscal Train Wreck' after All," *Business Week*, October 12, 1987.

p. 123 (1st): "The Senate's Anti-Deficit Duo," *U.S. News & World Report*, November 11, 1985.

p. 123 (2nd): "One Giant Step for Washington," *U.S. News & World Report*, December 23, 1985.

p. 124: "Mandate Steps to Balance the Budget," *U.S. News & World Report*, November 4, 1985.

p. 126: *Congressional Quarterly Almanac: 99th Congress, 1st Session, 1985*, vol. XLI (Washington, D.C.: Congressional Quarterly, 1986).

p. 130: Howard Gleckman, "The Bottom Line: Gramm-Rudman Isn't Working," *Business Week*, April 10, 1989.

pp. 137, 138: "Up in Arms," *Time*, December 20, 1993.

p. 140 (1st): Seth Mydans, "In California, a Lab for the Brady Bill Has No Winner," *The New York Times*, November 24, 1993.

pp. 140 (2nd), 143: Gordon Witkin, "Should You Own a Gun?" *U.S. News & World Report*, August 15, 1994.

BIBLIOGRAPHY

"Are We a Nation of Cowards?" *Newsweek*, November 5, 1993.

Berger, Raoul. "On Wars and Treaties: The Constitution Is Clear Enough." *Nation*, March 26, 1973.

Blinder, Alan S. "Balance the Budget—but Not with an Amendment." *Business Week*, July 27, 1987.

Boskin, Michael J. *Too Many Promises: The Uncertain Future of Social Security*. Homewood, Ill.: Dow Jones-Irwin, 1986.

"Broken Clock." *New Republic*, September 10 and 17, 1990.

Bruns, Roger A. *Preacher: Billy Sunday and Big-Time American Evangelism*. New York: Norton, 1992.

Calleo, David P. *The Bankrupting of America: How the Federal Budget Is Impoverishing the Nation*. New York: William Morrow, 1992.

"Congress Sends Nixon a Message." *Newsweek*, November 19, 1973.

Davidson, Osha Gray. *Under Fire: The NRA and the Battle for Gun Control*. New York: Henry Holt and Company, 1993.

Davis, Kenneth S. *FDR: The New Deal Years, 1933-1937: A History*. New York: Random House, 1979.

"The Debate on Civil Rights: Senator Humphrey vs. Senator Thurmond." *U.S. News & World Report*, March 30, 1964.

Fey, Harold E. "Politics and the Elderly: Toward a Sharing of Resources." *The Christian Century*, December 14, 1988.

Fisher, Louis. *Presidential War Power*. Lawrence: University Press of Kansas, 1995.

Friedrich, Otto. "A Bad Idea Whose Time Has Come." *Time*, February 3, 1986.

Gleckman, Howard. "The Bottom Line: Gramm-Rudman Isn't Working." *Business Week*, April 10, 1989.

Goodman, James A. "Presidential Battalions: The Power of the 'Undeclared War.'" *Nation*, February 14, 1976.

Gordon, John Steele. "Farewell to Taft-Hartley: The Great, Heroic American Labor Movement—How It Became Obsolete." *American Heritage*, October 1994.

Harbrecht, Douglas A. "Gramm-Rudman Looks More Than Ever Like a Pipe Dream." *Business Week*, July 6, 1987.

"How President's War Powers Are Cut." *U.S. News & World Report*, November 19, 1973.

Kobler, John. *Ardent Spirits: The Rise and Fall of Prohibition*. New York: Putnam, 1973.

Kotlikoff, Laurence J., *Generational Accounting: Knowing Who Pays, and When, for What We Spend*. New York: The Free Press, 1992.

Lawrence, David. "The Big Change." *U.S. News & World Report*, March 30, 1964.

"LBJ and Congress: The Next 100 Days." *U.S. News & World Report*, March 30, 1964.

Lehman, John. *Making War*. New York: Charles Scribner's Sons, 1992.

Lopez, Eduard A. "Déjà Views" *New Republic*, April 22, 1991.

Louchheim, Katie, ed. *The Making of the New Deal: The Insiders Speak*. Cambridge, Mass.: Harvard University Press, 1983.

McKinley, Charles, and Robert W. Frase. *Launching Social Security: A Capture-and-Record Account, 1935-1937*. Madison: University of Wisconsin Press, 1970.

Magnusson, Paul. "Gramm-Rudman Isn't a 'Fiscal Train Wreck' after All." *Business Week*, October 12, 1987.

"Mandate Steps to Balance the Budget." *U.S. News & World Report*, November 4, 1985.

Moley, Raymond. *The First New Deal*. New York: Harcourt, Brace & World, 1966.

"Mood of America in Election Year." *U.S. News & World Report*, March 30, 1964.

Musil, Robert K. "Congressional Giveaway: Troops for a Five-Star President." *Nation*, February 28, 1976.

Mydans, Seth. "In California, a Lab for the Brady Bill Has No Winner." *The New York Times*, November 24, 1993.

"New Deal for America's Employers." *Business Week*, June 28, 1947.

"One Giant Step for Washington." *U.S. News & World Report*, December 23, 1985.

Patterson, James T. *Mr. Republican: A Biography of Robert A. Taft.* Boston: Houghton Mifflin, 1972.

"The Rise of Citizen Militias." *U.S. News & World Report*, August 15, 1994.

"Senate Won't Make 'Tough Decisions' on Tax Reform." *U.S. News & World Report*, November 18, 1985.

"The Senate's Anti-Deficit Duo." *U.S. News & World Report*, November 11, 1985.

Shelar, Jeffrey L., et al. "Nothing but Tough Choices." *U.S. News & World Report*, November 25, 1985.

Thornton, Mark. "Prohibition's Failures: Lessons for Today." *USA Today*, March 1992.

"Toward a New System for Choosing a President." *U.S. News & World Report*, May 11, 1970.

Truman, Margaret. *Harry S. Truman.* New York: William Morrow, 1973.

"Up in Arms." *Time*, December 20, 1993.

Whalen, Charles W., and Barbara Whalen. *The Longest Debate: A Legislative History of the 1964 Civil Rights Act.* Cabin John, Md.: Seven Locks Press, 1985.

White, Theodore H. "Direct Elections: An Invitation to National Chaos." *Life*, January 30, 1970.

Witkin, Gordon. "Should You Own a Gun?" *U.S. News & World Report*, August 15, 1994.

INDEX

Coast Guard, U.S., 27
Colby, William, 114
Committee on Economic
    Security, 34, 37
Communists, 54, 57
Congress, U.S.: houses of, 7-9;
    powers of, stated in
    Constitution, 15, 102-103,
    104, 105, 107, 109, 110, 111,
    120; role of, in declaring
    war, 99-100, 101-103, 104,
    105-106, 107, 109, 110, 111,
    113-114; role of, in setting
    national budget, 116, 120,
    123, 124, 127
Congress of Industrial
    Organizations (CIO), 63
Constitution, U.S., 44, 66, 74,
    86; amendments to, 13, 15-
    16, 18, 25, 29, 66-67, 82, 90,
    125-126, 127, 130, 134, 135,
    138; powers granted by, 15,
    17, 18, 72, 73-74, 102-103,
    104, 105, 106-107, 108-109,
    110, 111, 120, 124, 127, 138;
    rights guaranteed by, 17, 18,
    53, 65, 70, 72, 73, 77, 134,
    135, 138, 146, 147
Constitutional Convention
    (1787), 86
Crusaders, 28
Cuba, 101

defense spending, 121, 123,
    124
deficit spending, 115-117, 118,
    120-121, 122, 124, 125, 129,
    130. See also national debt
Delahanty, Thomas, 133
Democratic Party, 9, 10, 71,
    80, 87, 108, 123, 138;
    presidential candidates of,
    82, 83, 84, 97; senators
    members of, 13, 34, 55, 68,
    74, 75, 99, 115, 119, 121,
    126, 144, 146
direct election: of president,

86, 90, 92, 94, 97; of
    senators, 90. See also popular
    vote
discrimination, 70, 72, 74-76,
    80; against African
    Americans, 65-66, 67-68, 70,
    72, 76, 80
districts represented by
    Congress, 8-9
drugs, 30
dry states, 15, 21, 22

Eagleton, Thomas, 99, 110,
    112
Eighteenth Amendment, 25,
    28, 29
Eisenhower, Dwight D., 71
elderly people, 9, 32, 33, 34,
    36; affected by Great
    Depression, 31, 32;
    retirement of, 36, 40, 44;
    social security assistance to,
    31-32, 36-37, 43, 44, 46
electoral college, bill to amend:
    failure of, 97; opposition to,
    91-94; support of, 86-88, 90
electoral-college system, 81-82;
    electors in, 81; history of,
    82-83, 84, 86; problems
    caused by, 82-83, 84, 86, 87,
    88, 97-98
Emancipation Proclamation,
    66, 70
employers: power of, 48-49,
    52, 56, 58; rights of, under
    Taft-Hartley bill, 47, 53-54,
    56, 64
equal rights, 9, 67, 68, 70, 72,
    73, 80. See also civil rights

Farmer, James, 67
federal government: deficit of,
    46, 115-117, 118, 120-121,
    122, 124, 125, 129, 130;
    powers of, 15, 17, 18, 72, 73-
    76; responsibilities of, 15,
    37-38, 56-57, 72, 136; and
    social security program, 35,

38, 39, 45, 46
filibuster, 97, 145
Ford, Gerald, 107-108
Fourteenth Amendment, 66-67, 70
freedom of speech, 53

Gascon, David, 140
German Americans, 17
Goldwater, Barry, 74, 79
Gramm, Phil, 115, 116, 124, 128
Gramm-Rudman-Hollings bill, 115-116, 119; effect of, 129-130; opposition to, 119-122, 124; passage of, 129; support for, 122-125
Great Depression, 27, 31, 32, 33, 39, 50
Grenada, 113
Gulf of Tonkin resolution, 102
gun control, 131-132, 133-134, 135-141, 143, 147; opposition to, 134, 135-138; support of, 132-133, 134, 138-141, 143

Haiti, 114
Hamilton, Alexander, 106-107
Hamilton, Lee, 130
handguns, 131, 133, 137, 142, 146; possession of, regulated by Brady bill, 131-132, 135, 138, 139, 144, 146-147; used in violent crimes, 131, 132, 133, 137-138, 139-140, 141, 143, 146
Harrison, Benjamin, 83, 84
Hart, Gary, 121
Hartley, Fred, 47, 48, 57
Hayes, Rutherford B., 82-83, 84, 86
Hinckley, John, 132, 133
Hobson-Sheppard resolution, 15
Hollings, Ernest, 115, 121, 128
House of Representatives, U.S., 6, 7-8, 9, 25; bills

passed by, 43, 61, 67, 68, 71, 85, 113, 134, 146; presidential elections decided in, 82, 85, 86, 87, 98
Hruska, Roman, 93
Humphrey, Hubert H., 68, 72, 73, 78, 83, 85

Industrial Revolution, 48
Industrial Workers of the World, 49
integration, school, 67, 71

Jackson, Andrew, 82, 83, 86
Javits, Jacob, 99
Jefferson, Thomas, 86
Jim Crow laws, 67
Johnson, Lyndon, 68, 70, 77, 78, 79, 102, 103, 106
Jones, Mary Harris "Mother," 49
Justice Statistics, Bureau of, 137

Kastenmeier, Robert, 71
Kellermann, Arthur, 140, 141
Kennedy, Edward, 118, 119
Kennedy, John F., 68, 70, 76, 91-92, 101
Kennedy, Robert, 76
King, Martin Luther, Jr., 67, 68, 69, 71, 77
Kleck, Gary, 137, 140, 143
Klineberg, Stephen, 138
Koh, Harold, 110
Kohl, Herb, 144
Korean War, 101, 102

Labor-Management Relations bill. See Taft-Hartley bill
La Guardia, Fiorello, 18
Landon, Alf, 38
LaPierre, Wayne, 137
Lawrence, David, 75
Lincoln, Abraham, 66, 70, 71
Little Rock, Arkansas, school integration in, 71
Long, Huey, 33, 34

ABOUT THE AUTHOR

NATHAN AASENG is an award-winning author of over 100 fiction and nonfiction books for young readers. He writes on subjects ranging from science to business, government to sports. Aaseng's books for The Oliver Press include *Great Justices of the Supreme Court*, *America's Third-Party Presidential Candidates*, *Genetics: Unlocking the Secrets of Life*, *You Are the Supreme Court Justice*, *You Are the President*, *You Are the President II*, *You Are the General*, *You Are the General II*, *You Are the Corporate Executive*, and the upcoming titles, *You Are a Member of the Jury* and *Treacherous Traitors*. He lives in Eau Claire, Wisconsin, with his wife and children.

Photo Credits

Photographs courtesy of: cover (background), p. 69, National Archives; cover (bottom right), pp. 119, 128, 136, 142, 144, U.S. Senate; pp. 6, 8, 16, 20, 23, 26, 28, 33, 38, 42, 46, 48, 49, 60, 79, 83 (left), 84 (top right and left, bottom left), 87, 101, 109, 145, Library of Congress; p. 10 (top), the National Democratic Party; p. 10 (bottom), the National Republican Party; p. 24, Archives Division—Texas State Library; pp. 25, 30, 32, 51, 58, 62, 78, 83 (right), 84 (bottom right), Minnesota Historical Society; p. 34, Louisiana Collection, State Library of Louisiana; Baton Rouge, Louisiana; p. 43, Franklin Delano Roosevelt Library; p. 55, Harry S. Truman Library; p. 63, AFL-CIO; p. 68, Birmingham Public Library; p. 71, Dwight D. Eisenhower Library; p. 75, South Caroliniana Library; p. 91, John F. Kennedy Library; p. 93, Nebraska State Historical Society; p. 96, Indiana State Library; p. 98, United We Stand America, Inc.; p. 102, MacArthur Memorial; p. 106, Yoichi R. Okamoto, LBJ Library Collection; p. 112, Missouri State Archives; pp. 123, 139, U.S. House of Representatives; pp. 126, 129, 132, 133, Ronald Reagan Library; p. 147, Handgun Control, Inc.